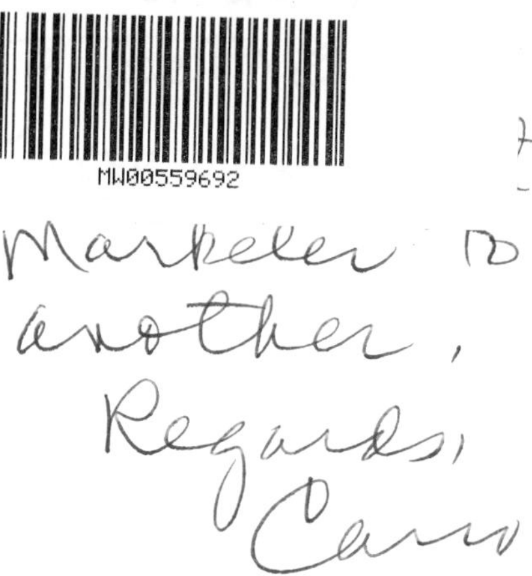
MW00559692
Marketer to
another,
Regards,
Carro

# THE SMARTASS MARKETER'S HANDBOOK

## A Guide to B2B Marketing with Attitude

Carro Susan Ford

# THE SMARTASS MARKETER'S HANDBOOK

**A Guide to B2B Marketing with Attitude**



Published in the United States by
Carro Ford Communications, LLC – Winchester, Kentucky

ISBN 978-0-692-31033-5 (paperback)
ISBN 978-0-692-31034-2 (eBook)
Printed in the United States of America

# TABLE OF CONTENTS

*For all the smartass marketers with whom I've had the pleasure of working (and playing), you know who you are.*

# FOREWORD

My background in marketing is deep, and that experience gets put to use at Forrester Research. As Vice President and Principal Analyst serving Chief Marketing Officers (CMOs), I provide strategic guidance to help clients succeed in the age of the customer. CMOs seek me out when they need an accomplished business-to-business (B2B) marketing expert with global experience in the full marketing mix in both Fortune 500 and early-stage companies. I help clients tackle business issues through customer insight-based, go-to-market strategies that span both digital and traditional channels.

So I can't deny that I know a lot about marketing. Having served as a senior-level marketer for over 25 years, I've had responsibility on par with the CMOs I now advise. I continue to live and breathe marketing through both research and by counseling clients, who are primarily companies of $500 million plus and include the world's best known brands.

Carro Ford and I first worked together in marketing about 15 years ago when I accepted a senior position at Océ North America (a Canon company.) She was part of a small group of accomplished marketers that I inherited with the new job. I enjoyed the entire team dynamic, which was a combination of direct employees and virtual contractors. They all brought different skills sets, and together we did what was needed to go to market in an integrated way on behalf of customers. The entire team created content with a consistency lacking in today's market.

Since I trusted her, when I went to another senior position at Ryder System, I took Carro and several of the freelance contractors with me. The skill set we had established translated well to the needs of a completely different B2B industry. Carro added value to my marketing teams, and now her book can bring value to yours.

With 20 years in corporate marketing and over 15 as a consultant with dozens of clients, she has "street cred" when it comes to knowing what works in day-to-day B2B marketing. She's been there, done that, and she has poured all of her experience into this practical handbook. If you want to save time and avoid trial and error, the ideas and tips in this book give you a clear path to final deliverables.

Sure, you'll find other marketing books out there, but they focus on other skills, like what to do in your first 100 days, or what it takes to be an effective CMO. This book fills a gap in B2B marketing literature. B2B is a very different animal from business-to-consumer (B2C ) marketing, and Carro has written a tactical book that will come in handy for B2B marketers at all stages of their game. It will help rookie marketers, as well as those who come into the job from a non-marketing background. Even experienced marketers can expand their tool set with ideas to use right away.

All too often, B2B marketers limit themselves to a sales support-oriented approach. They struggle to put different programs together and align with the customer lifecycle. For various reasons, they lack practical experience and know-how to multi-task their marketing efforts and explore new areas. Anything that lays out what they need to do is helpful, and this book does that for you in many ways.

While Carro doesn't explore big-picture strategy, she does provide in-depth micro-strategies for some of the most important tools in your B2B marketing toolkit. For the B2B marketer, this book comes in at a different level, the day-to-day desktop level where people grind out the pieces that go into a marketing strategy. It's a roadmap to specific results vs. leadership how-to.

This book gives you the tools and technique to be successful with a lot of marketing tools, from case studies and press relations, to industry awards and webinars. You may not become the CMO, but you'll be a better hands-on marketer.

I'm honored to write this foreword, because knowing Carro as I do, I believe you'll find something you can use and profit from in this book. It's all about experience and knowing where to focus. That's what got me where I am, and that's what got Carro where she is. Now enjoy your experience of exploring page after page of B2B marketing advice and wisdom, and get on the fast track to where you need to be.

**Sheryl Pattek**
Vice President, Principal Analyst
Serving Chief Marketing Officers (CMOs)
Forrester Research
spattek@forrester.com
http://blogs.forrester.com/sheryl_pattek

---

*About Sheryl Pattek*

*For over 25 years, Sheryl has been a strategic marketing practitioner and B2B expert. Before joining Forrester, she held senior roles in a diverse range of companies. She's led high-performing teams in logistics, transportation, software, software-as-a-service, technology and telecommunications industries.*

*Her expertise includes brand and product management, customer relationship management, lead generation, marketing automation, content marketing and digital marketing strategies. Well versed in customer analytics, retention and loyalty, she understands the importance of positive customer experiences.*

*She is a well-regarded speaker and moderator at such venues as the Forbes CMO Summit, The CMO Club, CMO Exchange, Argyle CMO Conferences, Direct Marketing Association Executive Summit, Dell World, and Marketing Operations Executive Summit.*

# INTRODUCTION

> *Confidence is the willingness to be as ridiculous, luminous, intelligent, and kind as you really are, without embarrassment.*
>
> — **Susan Piver,** Author, *How Not to Be Afraid of Your Own Life*

## The Many Names of Marketing: 40 Ways to Say I Want You

### What Snow and Marketing Have in Common

You may wonder, how are smartass and marketing even remotely connected? You'll be amazed at all the names we give our craft. They say the Eskimo culture has anywhere from ten to a hundred words for snow. Although that's a charming idea, it's not actually true. But did you know that the marketing culture has many times that many words for its trade? That is true, but is it necessary?

### Too Much Marketing

Search "marketing types" and you get literally millions of results. Wikipedia carries 81 pages for the entry of "types of marketing." I asked a few marketing veterans for input, did some Googling, and came up with dozens of types of marketing, some I'd never heard of.

Megamarketing? Reality marketing? Who knew?

Large vocabularies in specialized fields are not unusual. I understand the need for a few hyponyms, but does this seem excessive? You're targeting consumers? Okay, you're a B2C marketer. Sending mailers? Great, you're doing direct. As social media has taken hold, even more marketing terms have, too. There's viral, social, e and search marketing, and now the most popular kid in marketing school — mobile. Of course, there are the old standbys like one-to-one, guerilla, transpromo and integrated. Didn't these sound so progressive a few years ago?

### 40 Types of Marketing and Counting

Here is a partial list of the types of marketing we inflict on our target audiences. Disclaimer: This is not a definitive list by any means. I don't know if that's good or bad.

Affiliate
Article
Attraction
B2B
B2C
Brand
Cause
Channel
Content
Database
Digital
Direct
Email
Franchise
Green
Guerilla
Inbound
Influence
Integrated
International
Internet
Loyalty
Matrix
Mobile
Multi-channel
Multilevel
Non-profit
One-to-one
Outbound
Permission
Product
Niche
Relationship
Search
Social media
Target
Transpromo
Vertical
Viral
Word of mouth

### It's All Good

You probably have to be in marketing to remotely care that there are so many different names for what we do. I guess it comes down to the fact that marketing is such a versatile strategy. I just wonder if we risk diluting the message and value of our profession by splintering our contributions into so many categories?

But what I didn't see on this list was *Smartass Marketing*. That's when I knew I owed it to my people to write this book.

Some definitions call a smartass an annoying know-it-all. I think it's become a more affectionate term reserved for people who aren't afraid to say what they think. These smart alecs entertain us with the right combination of sarcasm, snark and spark. Clever or offbeat wise-guy commentary makes us pause and think, and when it's backed by perception and credibility, we can get away with it.

The best marketing teams I've worked with have been made up of cynical, but funny groups of smart marketers. The copywriters, graphic designers, supervisors, traffic people: the troops in the trenches who know exactly what they're doing, but maneuver through obstacle courses of marketing-challenged management, sales finger pointing, mid-year budget cuts and stock-obsessed CEOs. Gallows humor and occasional offsite gatherings with adult beverages were survival mechanisms that got us through and kept us bonded as effective teams.

This handbook is for anyone who wants the credibility to be a smartass marketer – the one who says things with bite and does things with attitude. By nature, I'm something of a smartass myself, albeit a low-key and sometimes unintentional one, but smartass nonetheless. To be a good smartass, you must be comfortable in your own skin and confident in your thinking. I think I can help you achieve this, at least as it relates to B2B marketing.

My goal is that everyone who reads this becomes a smarter marketer, whether you've been at the craft a long time or just getting started on your smartass career. May every chapter bring at least one idea you can use. The tips can be adapted to almost any B2B industry, and most don't cost much if anything to do.

The handbook starts by examining some of the raw materials of marketing, the most basic elements of customers, strategy and content, but mainly customers. Without customers, there wouldn't be any need for marketers. Everything we do as marketers should be informed by some kind of strategy, but it need not be complex. I almost named this handbook "Simple Marketing" for a reason. Then, especially to drive the B2B sales process, we've got to have content, all kinds of content. This is where you tell your story, provide useful information, germinate new ideas and make your company stand out. That overused phrase about the nobility of content is true. It's no coincidence that I got my start as a copywriter. In fact, there's a bonus section in the Appendix with tips on launching a freelance writing career. Someone has to create all this stuff, and it's steady employment if you're good at it.

The bulky mid-section of this handbook is devoted to things you should have in your marketer's toolkit. My intent wasn't to focus so much on the "what" of these tools, but the "how." You'll find lists, tips, examples and advice for working with content and making connections. There's even a chapter on a tool you might neglect sometimes – you! If there's one thing I've learned, it's that there is usually no one way to do anything. Marketing "rules" are sketchy at best. Trust yourself and try stuff.

There's a lot of marketing I haven't covered in this book, and not because the topics aren't important. Things like inbound marketing, blogging, search optimization, collateral, web copy and copywriting in general are admittedly neglected. At some point, I had to draw the line and get this darn book out. Perhaps I'll have the time and energy to cover in a future book those topics that missed the cutoff.

I think what has been included will still be very helpful to you. Writing this material was such a joy, because for once, I didn't have to get approval from anyone else. Not the director of communications, not the vice president of marketing. It was all mine. And in the end, I was surprised at how much I knew. Now I want you to make it all yours. From one smartass to another.

**Carro Susan Ford**

# CHAPTER 1

## There's Someone I Want You to Meet

 *Think like a customer.* 

— **Paul Gillin,** Author,
*The New Influencers*

By definition, marketing doesn't exist without someone to market to. What would be the point? Yet this is one of the biggest mistakes busy B2B marketers make. We don't spend enough time talking to customers. We have our personas and our message maps and the other crutches that we think make us customer experts, but too often the marketing crew stays locked up in the corporate tower. We guess. We assume. We miss the mark.

Do whatever it takes to spend time with the people who buy your stuff. Wrangle a shift at a conference. Beg to ride around with a sales manager for a day. Make connections however you can. Then, you'll be ready to take the next step.

### Put Your Customers on Your Marketing Team

Nothing says "credibility" like a satisfied customer. Whenever you use a customer story or quote in your marketing, those efforts carry more weight than almost anything else you can do. And it's not just new prospects who pay attention. Hard-to-impress editors, analysts, bloggers and other influencers put far more stock into what your customers say about you than what you claim.

## Interview Smartly for Mega-Content

If you plan it right and ask good questions, you can capture enough content for a variety of uses from just one good interview and without imposing on the customer's time and good will. There are many ways to work these customer experiences, perspectives and opinions into high-value marketing content. Here's a start:

1. **Case studies** – Traditional tools but still marketing "gold." Open with a story that sets the stage. Use lots of customer quotes to describe the problem and how you solved it. Quote more than one person in the company, if you can.
2. **Customer councils, user conferences and groups** – A large-scale team effort, but great for networking and word-of-mouth marketing. Starting small is a good plan if it's your first one. You can use these opportunities for press releases, photos, quote gathering, schmoozing and more.
3. **Quotes** – Constantly replenish a stockpile of great, approved quotes - along with the customer's name and title. If you can't reveal the name, at least use the title and industry that's represented. You can collect quotes from case studies, user meetings, trade shows and other opportunities and add them to the quote library. Organize quotes by vertical market, types of problems solved, benefits, and your own product lines. You'll have them on hand for press releases, blogs, articles, editor requests, tweets and more.
4. **Guest blogs** – Invite customers to write a blog for you, or to put their name on a ghostwritten post. You'll have to come up with a "what's in it for them" reason. One might be that a blog gives them greater visibility as a leader with editors and analysts who follow your corporate blog. On the flip side, see if blogging customers will let you do a guest post for them. The angle could be a new approach to a problem, and how this customer has taken the industry lead in that direction.

5. **Tweets** – Tweet about customers who are successful with your products and share links to their case studies. Focus on the problem, not on your company. For example: "Find out why Company X no longer has to wait days to get new acct approvals. [Link to case study.]" If you can get customers to tweet about you (i.e. the problem that got solved), even better. Set up a #hashtag with a term relevant to the problem that is being solved, such as #digitaldocuments.

6. **White paper examples** – White papers, executive reports, guides and eBooks are more interesting and credible when they include real examples. Draw on your case studies for suitable references for your white paper. As a courtesy, let your customers know they are being featured, even if they previously approved the case study. And if they shy from going public, reference them as a generic title from the "whatever" industry.

7. **Trade shows and conferences speakers** – Conferences love to have real customers speak, instead of vendors. Get these efforts going far in advance of the show. It's a diplomatic coup to get a customer to agree to send someone to speak on your company's behalf. Be prepared to pay their travel expenses. Offer to help develop their presentation. Do whatever it takes to make the assignment easy on them.

8. **Special booth guests** – On rare occasions, you can get customers to appear in your trade show booth. You won't position it as "come work a shift," but more like having a book signing. Market it as "come spend time with representative of company X and find out how they cut their processing workflow by half," or something like that. Play it up with signage on site, pre-show promotions, tweets, blogs and more. Schedule editors to come during the show for interviews.

9. **Ads** – Customers make great ads, and they like seeing themselves in print. Be sure to have some reprints framed to give to the customer as gifts. Think of it as the billboard or Twitter version of their case study.

*Not only do you want your customers on your marketing team, you want them in your* ***plan****. In fact, they* ***are*** *the plan.*

## Make a Customer Plan, Not a Marketing Plan

### Why Writing a "Marketing Plan" Doesn't Work

Imagine it's time to prepare for your annual marketing plan, but wait. First, I have a confession. I think it's an exercise in futility to write marketing plans for more than three months out. Competitors surprise you. Budgets get cut. Product launches stall. End-of-quarter sales fire drills demolish your priorities. God and the market laugh when marketing mortals make "plans." Your plans will be screwed up, so be prepared to be flexible is all I'm saying.

### Think Three Months at a Time

More realistic for many companies is a flexible, rolling three-month plan, that yes, in a way, you make up as you go along. But then, isn't that how marketing works anyway?

Some fixed landmarks will help you steer a little during the year: a couple of must-attend trade shows. That product launch that has to happen in the second quarter. The sales plan dependent on x-number of unit sales. You won't be totally rudderless.

### It's Not a Marketing Plan

So, make a plan? Don't make a plan? Then what's the point of all this? I suggest building your marketing plan around the one thing that stays constant. Think of it as a ***Customer Plan***, not a

Marketing Plan. Don't approach it from what you will do, but how can you encourage engagement with the right customers? What do they care about? How will you reach out to them? What will you say, and when? What are they planning to do in their own businesses in the coming year? How can you help?

All your traditional and social media and marketing efforts will still have a place, but the framework is built around catering to the customer. Ace your customers, and the plan will come.

It's folly, of course, to expect a successful marketing effort without an actual marketing plan, the stuff you are going to do. I know that. I'm just being a smartass.

### Hitting the Sales Plateau?

I had an energizing discussion with a new client recently. We wanted to set up the first ever marketing strategy for this already successful business. Why marketing now, when they have never done any and seem to be going just fine? As the CEO put it, it's "easy" to take a business from $1 million to $2 million, and then from $2 million to $4 million, but after that, the leaps get harder to pull off. It's at that point smart entrepreneurs start looking for new ideas, and marketing counts as a new idea if you've never used it before. If you're way beyond the entrepreneur stage, try to go back to that mindset and imagine marketing as a blank slate.

### No Question Is Dumb

What questions could you ask to develop a marketing plan? Try these for starters. They may be all you'll need.

### Build on What You Have

Q What strengths have gotten you to this point?

Q What markets have been most profitable, and what is it you offer them?

- Q Will these markets carry you forward, or is it time to tap into some new ones?
- Q What kind of customer information do you have in your database?
- Q How many customers do you have? How many do you want?
- Q Will growth come from new clients or from greater share of current customers?
- Q Where do you want to focus to drive your next level of growth – what markets?
- Q What new products or services are planned for the next 3-6 months?

**Connecting with Customers and Their Problems**

- Q Where do your leads come from now?
- Q Who do you work with in your customers' organizations? Who makes the decision to bring you in?
- Q What are the top problems you solve for clients?
- Q How do you help them solve problems? How do you do that better than the alternative?
- Q What is the alternative?
- Q If your clients didn't have you, what would they do to solve these problems?
- Q Turning weakness into strength – what are your perceived weaknesses and how do you counter them?

**Exploring the Publicity Landscape**

- Q What trade journals and websites provide good information about your industry?
- Q What trade shows and conferences do you and your customers attend?

- Have you done much speaking at industry events?
- Do you have customers who would be willing to participate in case studies and press releases?
- What industry associations are important to your current markets?

## The Gift of Information

- Do different markets like different things about your company? Or is your appeal market-neutral?
- What kind of information best helps your sales people close the deal? What makes the customer say "Ah hah!"?
- If you could educate your customers about certain topics, those topics would be...
- What kinds of questions do customers ask your customer service department?

## Forget What You Know About Marketing

Remember what I said about the blank slate. Get Zen and clear your mind. Forget all your assumptions and start developing your "customer plan" as if anything is possible. It often is.

# CHAPTER 2
## Your Marketing Wardrobe

> *Many a small thing has been made large by the right kind of advertising.*
>
> — **Mark Twain,** Author, *A Connecticut Yankee in King Arthur's Court*

Think of your annual marketing program as your company's wardrobe. Invest in a few versatile content pieces that you can wear over and over in many ways, and you'll be prepared for any selling occasion.

### What Does Your Marketing Wardrobe Say About Your Business?

Nothing says chic like a well-dressed marketing strategy. What does yours say about you? High-energy over-achiever? Unimaginative trend follower? Out-of-date communicator? Confident iconoclast? Check your closet and see if it's time to update some of those items you've been wearing around lately.

#### Dress for Success

- **Professionally written white paper** – Great for formal occasions like conferences, or casual events like website visits. A good white paper isn't cheap, but you can get a lot of wear out of your investment. Choose a topic that will get the most thought leadership attention for you in your target markets.

- **Case studies** – Choose customer stories that have impressive, quantifiable results, or those that focus on a key target market. And spend some money on some flattering photos, even if you have to pay for a photographer. It will be worth it to make your case studies look more stylish.
- **Blogging** – I know, I know. You have lots of reasons not to blog, but none of those look that good on you. Get over it and just start. If you can't think of 300 words of weekly wisdom to share with your customers and industry, I have to wonder what you do have to offer. It's tough blog love, baby. Don't worry about wardrobe malfunctions.
- **Press releases** – This will be one of the staples of your marketing wardrobe that you'll turn to again and again. But remember, press releases are like blogging – you don't want to do just one. If you can deliver just one release a month, you will have done a nice job of getting out your company's message.

After you've got these basics in your marketing wardrobe, you can accessorize with things like webinars, LinkedIn posts and emailing. Even if you just spend time, thought and money on these core content pieces alone, your company will look smart and stand out from the crowd.

## Ideas to Build Your Contact List

Once you've got your marketing wardrobe looking stylish with pieces that play up your best features, you'll want to share some of this awesomeness with your prospects, influencers and customers. Take a look at your email lists. Could they use a makeover?

It's always a surprise to me how unprepared companies are to tap into their own customer databases. Sometimes the data exists in different, disjointed silos. Sometimes emails are nonexistent or out of date. You may have better luck building up an email list of press and influencers, and we cover that later in the book.

As you execute your plan, and we *always* execute it, (poor plan, shot down in its prime) you won't get too far without running up against "The Brand." (Cue angelic chorus.) I'm sorry, but...

## BRANDING IS STUPID

IMHO, big branding initiatives and makeovers are a waste of a good marketing budget.

The big mistake I see corporate B2B marketers make with branding is nursing the illusion that you control it. You may call the brand your vision or your promise, but if you have a brand at all, it's defined by your customers and your market, not you.

Your company brand is organic, and the perception of it comes from the outside in. It's not something you create from design mock-ups and focus groups, and push out to the marketplace. The new logo, the new tagline and promise – that's just a wrapper. You cannot control your brand. You can influence it.

Think of some of the big brands – Apple, Gap, Virgin – they have a clear brand message (or used to), but do you think they defined it and made everyone agree that that's what it was? Hell no. They did their thing, did it memorably and consistently, and THAT became the brand. Anything else is just a marketing campaign.

### Do You Really Have a Brand?

Okay, here's the big test, in case you still have doubts. If you think there really is such a thing as a brand, ask your customer what your brand is. Ask them if they know what your brand promise is. I am willing to bet they have no frigging clue. And whatever they do throw out as an answer will probably have nothing to do with that brand promise and vision you slaved over for months.

Do what you're good at. Make your customers happy. You'll come out with a brand that means something.

## Does Your Brand Need a Tagline?

Company taglines can be brilliant. Some are funny. Some, obscure. Some, just plain stupid. But does the ultimate target – your customer – really give a darn?

Coming up with these little gems takes a lot of time. You hire the agency big guns. Or you lock the marketing team in a room with flip charts, Post-its, markers, coffee, bottled water and doughnuts. Let the brainstorming games begin.

But what does that really, really do for your brand?

## Taglines and Your Brand

Your tagline is your brand, you say. Really? You can embody your brand in less than ten words? Don't fool yourself. It may affect your company's "coolness factor" if you have a very clever tagline, but sales? I don't think so. Ask your customers if they even know what your tagline is.

I think the "priceless" campaign was American Express, but does that affect my use of that card? Not in the slightest. Does anyone say, I think I'll buy software from this company because they have that great tagline?

Brand is important, but it's ultimately something you don't have control over. You can say what you want your company brand to be, but unless everyone is on board with that, it's just a shell. Your brand is the consistent customer experience. A smart tagline isn't going to change that one way or another.

## What Taglines Are, What They Aren't

Taglines aren't permanent. They are the equivalent of a Twitter-sized advertising campaign. They can go viral and morph into something that becomes part of the culture. Blog per month $9, website per month $24. Platform to rant – priceless. Got Milk?

Got this? Got that? See what I mean? They are fun, but do you think more highly of the American Dairy Association?

## Taglines Aren't Easy

Every marketing writer knows, the shorter the copy, the harder it is to write. A good tagline will be one of the most difficult things to craft for your company. What do you want it to do? Is it for your customer, or for you? Of course, you can always pay an agency big bucks to come up with one for you.

If you're set on doing one, and I'm not really saying you shouldn't, then do it — but don't kid yourself that it's crucial to your marketing strategy. I used to think so. Confession time – I was one of those marketing directors who confined my team to a room to create a tagline by force. And we came up with some that were pretty good, but did it really affect the bottom line? Was it worth all the effort? Honestly, no.

## Enjoy Taglines, Just Don't Expect Too Much

I actually admire quite a few taglines, but I am attracted to them as someone who has an appreciation of clever words, not for their value as a marketing tool. Taglines I like share these qualities:

- Succinct
- Clever
- Directed to the customer benefit

Here are some that fit at least one of my criteria. Here's the true test: can you name the company that goes with each?

- *You are now free to move about the country.*
- *When it absolutely, positively has to be there overnight.*
- *It's not just for breakfast anymore.*
- *Australian for beer.*
- *Never let 'em see you sweat.*
- *American by birth. Rebel by choice.*

## If You Must Tag, Here Are Some Resources

If you insist on pursuing a tagline, here are some sites that you might find helpful:

- http://www.chomchomadvertising.com/360-most-famous-business-taglines/ Doesn't matter what your generation, you'll find something here to make you smile.
- http://www.taglineguru.com/ Actually a lot of good info about the tagline process.
- http://www.dailyblogtips.com/the-best-website-taglines-around-the-internet/ Snarky, clever taglines from websites.

## Taglines Serve the Company, Not the Customer

I've come to the conclusion that a tagline is not necessary for your business, or should I say, your customers. Taglines are more for internal satisfaction, than convincing someone they should buy from your company. If it makes you feel good to come up with a tagline, then do it. Happy marketers are good marketers. I'm sure that's being used as a tagline somewhere.

# CHAPTER 3

## Content. Content. Content.

*"Worry less about sounding professional and worry more about creating remarkable content that other humans can relate to."*

— **Ann Handley,** Chief Content Officer, *MarketingProfs*

This might be better called **Word. Word. Word**. We all know content is on the throne, but it's writers who keep it there. If you aren't a strong writer, fill your team with them and turn your group into a content machine. Word up.

### Content Marketing: It's a Gift

An insightful friend asked how many marketers really know what is meant by "content marketing." It's a buzzword used frequently, but for me, this buzzword actually means something. And so, I started to pound out my definition, in order to answer my colleague's question, but it felt hollow and wrong. Finally, I realized that's because so many others have already described it very well, and my efforts weren't necessary.

#### Advantages of Content Marketing

I realized I needed to focus on why I think it's such a valuable marketing concept and explain why I can't shut up about it. Here are some of the reasons I think every marketer today – B2B and B2C – should be thinking about content marketing:

- You can build relationships based on value.

- Repeatable – you can continually provide useful information.
- Interactive – people respond, you reply, they respond, you reply.
- Ideal for the online world.
- Suited to all types of media: print, electronic, video, podcast, webinars and more.
- It benefits recipients as much as the presenter.
- You can cover topics in appropriate and progressive detail.
- It fits into customer's buying process – stay in touch with the right level of info until they are ready to go to the next step.
- Easy to build in keywords and optimize for search for broader digital reach.
- People are more willing to give you their contact info for something of value.
- When done online, results are trackable and measurable.
- Can create a reputation for thought leadership in your niche and market.
- Very affordable. Whether you write it yourself or hire a copywriter, it's not a budget-buster.
- You get to call yourself a publisher, because you are one.
- Online means you can get new content out immediately in response to the market.
- You can repurpose, repurpose, repurpose.

### The Gift that Keeps on Giving

Think of content as a thoughtful present, a helpful gift. If the information is useful to the reader, they will remember where it came from. When it's time for a purchase, you will be one of the companies that come to mind.

Whether you're creating content in-house, or hiring a freelancer, you need to give them a starting point. The content brief is the traditional tool used to focus a content marketing project. If you're using outside resources, a good brief makes their job easier. It's only fair to give them the best guidance you can. If the brief is wonky, you're going to be doing a lot of rewriting. Try to get it right the first time. The next section provides some tips for doing that.

## Get Stronger Copy when You Start with a Content Brief

Companies and agencies often start projects with a Creative Brief – an overview of goals, target audiences, messaging, timing, delivery channel and so on. The Creative Brief typically includes details about the physical look and feel of the piece. That's certainly necessary for the team, including your project's writer, but copywriters can do a better job when they have certain information from the start.

Getting good copy out of your copywriter depends not only on their writing skills, but also on their understanding of what you are after. If you don't know, they can't figure it out for you. (Well, maybe some of us can.) A good brief on the front end of any marketing project will contribute to fewer revisions and rewrites on the back end and faster speed to market.

### What Your Copywriter Wants to Know

Since I'm a copywriter, I've learned there are certain things I need to know about a project from a content perspective. Next time you think about a Creative Brief, consider including some of these questions, so the overview will also serve as a stronger Content Brief for your copywriter.

## The Basics

- Q What service, product or event are you promoting through this piece?
- Q Is this something new or does it introduce an existing product to a new audience?
- Q How would you describe the desired tone of the piece? Playful? Formal? Something else?
- Q Where and how will readers receive it? What is the medium or delivery channel, such as direct mail, email, web page, white paper or case study?
- Q What is the approximate length of the copy? Is it email length? Sales letter? Direct mailer? White paper?
- Q Is there a standard layout template to follow for this type of piece or content?
- Q What's the deadline for final copy? When is the piece scheduled for launch?

## The Resources

- Q Who is the topic expert in your company?
- Q Are there current customers who also might be appropriate to interview? Provide all contact info and clearance.
- Q Are there additional written background material or other resources that could be used?

## The Players

- Q Who is the internal point person for the project?
- Q Who owns this project in your company?
- Q What department has requested the project?
- Q Who will need to review and approve copy? Who will handle the review process?

- Q If you're an international company, will this content be used in other markets? What's the input and approval process? What about translations?

### The Readers

- Q Who is the target audience for this piece? Think in terms of title and industry.
- Q What does the reader already know about your company, product or service?
- Q What keywords and phrases are relevant for this audience/product/problem/market?
- Q What market trends, issues or opportunities related to this piece are impacting your target readers?
- Q Where is the reader in the sales process when they get this? Such as:
  - New prospect?
  - Current customer?
  - Knows the company, but not convinced yet to buy?

### The Value

- Q What problems will this information solve for the target audience?
- Q What are the top three to five messages of the piece?
- Q What features and benefits should be included?
- Q What is the background on the project? That is, why is it needed?

### The Outcome

- Q What do you want the reader to do/feel/know as a result of receiving this information?
- Q What's their motivation for doing this?

Having the answers to these questions will save time for your copywriter and speed time to market for your marketing projects and campaigns. Content will be closer to the goal sooner and require fewer revision cycles.

As you prepare your brief, don't use trite generalities and useless jargon. Be as specific as possible. You're not selling here. You are providing direction to a professional. The answers might also just help a struggling marketer think more strategically about the role of the content and about the outcome they want to achieve.

## Marketing Content: It's Okay to Lead with Fear

Why are marketers so afraid of fear? It's one of the strongest emotions known to man, and a great motivator. Isn't that what marketing is about? Motivation?

It happens often enough, but it still never ceases to puzzle me. I write what seems to be a persuasive bit of copy for a white paper or a brochure, and the client kicks it back as "too negative."

The copy rejections usually come when the opening paragraph describes the downside of a business problem. Companies losing revenue due to missed opportunities. Inefficient workflow dragging down productivity. Poor training impacting employee safety.

It's all too negative. Really? The reason customers buy your product is because they are dealing with something negative. They've got a business problem, a "challenge," speaking euphemistically. To them, it is scary. It's worrisome. It's a threat. Leading with this fear is actually a smart way to start your copy. Here's why:

## Set the Stage for the Selling Process

Notice how many news stories start with a personal story illustrating the broader topic of the article? They put a face to the problem. At this opening point in your copy, it's a bit early to bring in your products. You first must show you understand your customer's world and their problems. That gives you the right to talk about answers and alternatives.

Once you have your reader thinking and worrying about their business problem, the problem you solve, you have their attention. You have them in the right mindset for the next stage of your copy. Then it's time to switch gears and lead them into the realm of sweetness and light, the happy spot where customers chose your products and services, and everyone lives happily ever after.

## Let the Copy Pre-qualify the Reader

Use fear-based copy as a means of qualifying readers. If the problem you describe doesn't worry them, they probably don't have a need for what you offer. No point in wasting time.

## Get Inside the Buyer's Head

Don't lead with the pretty picture of where they will end up after buying your product. They probably aren't there yet. Where they are now is in a state of concern over a problem that needs to be fixed.

## Demonstrate Understanding

In Happy Marketing Land, we only write about positive things. Unfortunately, that's not the world of our customers. They've got a problem – don't be afraid to talk about that. It shows you get their world. Get real. Show your customers you understand the downside, the worse case scenario, but that you also know how to pull them out of the tailspin.

### Create a Home for Good Keywords

Leading with copy about a business problem is a good way to work in keywords for search marketing. What phrases do customers use to describe this problem? These are the same ones they will use when they do a search for something to help. Lead with the problem, and you can get those good keywords and phrases right up front where they count.

### Use Emotion to Capture Attention, Commitment and Interest

Emotions create a connection between the content and the viewer, and you do want to bond with this potential customer, right? Start with a picture of the threat, the risk. That gets attention. We recognize and are attracted to descriptions of our problems. Humans are drawn to reading about troubles and disasters.

If you lead with the happy stuff, you risk not capturing their attention. The role of the opening paragraph is to take the handoff from the headline and keep your reader engaged. If they recognize themselves and the reality of their life, interest is created, followed by a commitment to reading more.

### Embrace the Duality

It's okay to be negative sometimes, just as it's okay to be sad or mad. Without the bad, there can't be good. And that's not me talking. I think God or Buddha or somebody said it first. Without a problem, you can't sell a solution.

### FUD You

"Negative value marketing" isn't new. Case studies are frequently structured in the problem/solution/results formula. Same thing. You may also recall the FUD sales approach of Fear, Uncertainty and Doubt, often associated with IBM in days past. FUD typically refers to scaremongering to establish doubts about a competitor's product. Leading with the negative in your copy isn't exactly the same thing, but it does play on emotions and uncertainty. Clearly, IBM knew a thing or two about that. The "fear" copy I'm talking about is more along the lines of what's your greatest fear if you don't solve this problem?

### Face the Fear

Is it negative to point out the consequences of failing to find an answer to a nagging business problem? No, it's a set up for an alternative vision of what life looks like with an answer to the "challenge," as we euphemistically refer to these problems. I say it's realistic to write this way. Don't be afraid to tap into customers' fears, as long as you can suggest a way to make them go away – the fears, that is, not the customers.

While we're on the subject of euphemism, may I add a few words about words? I've already mentioned how important good writers are to good marketing. So are good words. Many words, not through their own faults, are no longer suitable for careers in marketing. Please retire them. Customers have seen these so many times, they don't see them any more, and that defeats your purpose.

## Thoughtful Words. Conscious Copywriting.

Seen any of these words lately in a brochure? Press release? Web page? Of course you have. Maybe I even put it there, and shame on me!

### Word Up

I should know this list by heart, since I am guilty of having used these tired, meaningless phrases. You can probably add a few favorites of your own, but then again, I'd rather you didn't. They get enough exposure as it is.

### Words to Kill

- Key
- Transform
- Explore (Who are we? Daniel Boone?)
- Optimize
- Value add
- Robust
- Feature-rich
- Leading edge
- Best in breed
- Quality
- Innovative
- Customer focus
- Customer delight
- Customer intimacy
- Laser focus
- Critical and its cousin, mission-critical
- Challenge and opportunity
- Solution – Oh, especially you, evil Solution!

## Enjoy in Moderation

I have a personal copywriting rule that I am loath to break. I am only allowed to use the word "solution" one time in any piece I compose. It is possible, and the limitation forces me to think of stronger, more specific words.

## Make It a Habit

Let's all agree – for one week, we won't use these phrases in our marketing copy, and we won't ask our writers to either. Friends don't let friends write crap.

# CHAPTER 4

## Marketing Toolkit – Influencer Relations

> *"Marketers need to build digital relationships and reputation before closing a sale."*
>
> — **Chris Brogan,** CEO, *Owner Media Group*

This is the first of the Marketing Toolkit sections that cover specific tactics you'll need as a Smartass Marketer. This chapter deals with what is often called PR – public relations or sometimes "Media Relation," and increasingly, "Influencer Relations." I'll use those terms interchangeably, but you can call it whatever you want. Just don't forget, it's not about what you want to talk about. It's about what those influencers want to know.

### Why Do You Need an Influencer Relations Strategy?

Since all good plans start with the objectives, consider these for your influencer relations program.

### Objectives:

- Generate successful influencer engagements that lead to coverage of these issues in your terms.
- Raise awareness about the impact these issues have on an enterprise and create urgency to learn more.
- Build credible awareness of your company as a short-list player who understands the issues and brings solutions in the context of those issues.

- Lead buyers into sales process through engagement with your content as a trusted resource.

**Persons of Influence**

Here's one truth you need to know about influence marketing. It's a lot of work, but don't be discouraged. A good, steady effort can deliver results that benefit your business. Eat the elephant one bite at a time, and you'll get there eventually. First, you have to find your influencers, but even before that, (pre-first, I guess) you have to find your focus. If your company has several categories where you want to cultivate influence or thought leadership, you may end up with more than one influencer group. If you are part of a marketing team, consider splitting these topics up among the group. Plenty of work to go around. I'm not going to get wrapped around the axle of advocate vs. influencer or paid vs unpaid. The focus here is to give you ways to find influencers organically yourself.

**Google Is Your Best Friend**

Make lists of the relevant terms that define your categories, and set up Google alerts for them. Set up Google alerts for your competitors and your own company. Just Google "Google Alerts" and follow the directions to start your list.

The email alerts that come daily to your inbox include a brief summary and a link to the full content. Often the alerts provide links to relevant press that you wouldn't have known about otherwise. You can see what bloggers and pubs cover your topics and what the relevant articles look like. You can also see what other companies are getting picked up and for what topics.

**Start a Master List**

As alerts come in, start a list of conferences, blogs, websites, forums, communities and magazines connected to the information the alerts bring to you. Also keep lists of people associated with good alerts, those whose names continue to come up. You can then look to Twitter and LinkedIn for deeper dives. See who these people follow on Twitter and what groups they belong to on LinkedIn. This will lead you to more names.

Make a spreadsheet or a Word table, if like me, spreadsheets make you queasy. Make notes about where you see these people appear: perhaps categories for blogs (theirs and others), conference speakers, number of Twitter followers, participation in LinkedIn groups.

At some point, you will just have to use your gut to decide if the candidates are true influencers. There's no magic formula. Some may drop off your list later; some may reappear – like quantum particles. Since this process takes so long, you won't be ready for the next step for a while. Allow yourself a few weeks to do all this. Remember, you're eating an elephant. But take heart. Along the way, you are going to learn a lot about your target topics and markets.

## Build a Press List from Scratch

The press, the journalists who cover your industry, represent a core group of influencers. If you don't have the bandwidth to do a broad influencer relations strategy right now, at least focus on your trade press.

The foundation of a good program is a well-connected media list. The Internet and digital communications have transformed the techniques we use to reach journalists, but you still sometimes need the traditional email list to distribute press releases, invitations and other information. If you can spend the time on it, you can build an awesome press list yourself. It's like any DIY project. Expect it to be time-consuming, but it's a good way to learn first hand what's available.

There are several ways to build a list. You could pay for one. A number of services will assemble a targeted list for you for a fee. If you are in a particularly niche-y market like commercial printing or utility marketing, most of what you get will be garbage, in my humble experience.

You could spend months or years collecting contacts and organically building a community of editors and analysts. If you've got the time, by all means, this is a great way to build a list of people who actually know who you are. When it comes to influencer lists, always be building.

## Other Sources for Influencer Ideas

### Customers Know Best

Ask your customers what they read. Ask your sales people to scope out offices and lobbies when they make sales calls. Do an inexpensive survey using SurveyMonkey or some other free tool.

### The Blogging Beast

Don't forget bloggers. Technorati is one resource for finding bloggers in your industry, but there are other sources. Fall back on Google and search. Trade journals and their websites are also home base for industry-specific bloggers. Writers often make it hard to get in direct contact with them, but try courting them through sincere and thoughtful posts, and perhaps the gates will open.

### I Spy

Go to competitors' websites, or partners or others in your industry. The good sites will post or link to articles about their companies. Add these to your list. Note who writes the articles. These people will need to go on your list.

# Kickstart Your Influencer List: Use a Conference Website

## Finding Influencers in a Niche Market

What if you need fast information about something outside your norm, such as a vertical market your company wants to enter? How do you find out who reaches and influences that audience? What if you're introducing a product to a new market, or ramping up a PR program for a company that hasn't had much of one before?

You could do lots of search and research, Googling and guessing, as you validate (or reject) one website after another. You could buy an iffy list.

But if you want to save time and kickstart a targeted media list in a niche market, the best free and fast resources are the trade shows and conferences that target your particular interest. You can learn a heck of a lot from conferences, and you don't even have to attend!

The information gleaned from a conference site can accelerate the growth of your media list for a specific market. Pick a healthy trade show, study its website, mailers and marketing, and learn a lot about your market influencers and what interests them — all without flashing an attendee badge even once.

## More Than You Would Expect

If you've never mined a conference website for research, you're missing out on free and available background information and contacts. You'll discover more than you might expect, even if it's just finding a URL that points your media research in the right direction. Having the right URLs avoids hours of false starts and research rat holes.

### Who Are the Conference Media Sponsors and Exhibitors?

The good thing is, with the conference website as your media ground zero, you have the links and typically some background immediately available to help move your media research along. And the information is usually fairly current, even if it's last year's press list. The main media sites themselves won't change that much. For starters, look for media sponsors and media exhibitors to see who has an interest in this segment. With niche media lists, it's not quantity you're after, it's quality.

### What's There? Who's There?

The program and agenda sections of a conference site tell you the top issues getting attention in your target market. By looking at the speakers and their topics, you can see who's an influencer on a particular subject. You even get a head start on how to talk about these issues by noting the terms used to describe sessions.

Move to the exhibitor and sponsor sections for a moment. Scan to see what media outlets have a presence. From there you can drill down on their websites for more contacts for your influencer list. Note competitors and other significant players. Jump over to the newsrooms on their sites to see if you can find any influencer names.

What else can you learn from a conference website? You can find and use background about people in the industry, such as:

- Speaker bios – Learn about industry pundits, luminaries and rock stars.
- Their Twitter feeds – If you Tweet, you'll understand.
- Bloggers covering the industry – Get insights into their interests.
- Reasons to reach out to all the above – What interests overlap with yours?

Another takeaway are the job titles. You can apply this to almost any B2B conference in any industry. Look at the job descriptions and departments used to sell the conference to the exhibitors and attendees. (Of course, the "decision makers" go to every show. That's a given.)

You can use these descriptors in several ways:

- To target your search and social marketing
- To find LinkedIn groups that are relevant to this market
- In your marketing content to connect with the reader
- In your PR outreach to show editors and journalists you're relevant to their audience

## The Influencer in the Exhibitor Guide

Use the conference guide to scope out the competition and identify potential partners who are influencers (or who consider themselves so.) Look at the product categories in the online exhibit guide. What categories do competitors choose for their listings? Look at the program agenda. Who's giving presentations? On what topics? Perhaps you can even build a "competitive persona" based on some of this information. Study their marketing, releases and messages and get a sense of how to approach this market, or how to stand apart from the competition.

## Ask for the Show Press List

Ask the conference PR manager or marketing director for the list of pre-registered press. Explain that you want it in order to develop your interest in the conference "as an exhibitor." Even if they offer last year's list, take it. The media won't change that much, and what you really want is a website and an email. (You'd be amazed at how many sites make finding the editor's email next to impossible.)

### Get Social with Your Influencers

Immerse yourself in the conference's social media marketing, even if just temporarily. You can always turn the hose off after your research is done. Get on the conference RSS feed, Twitter account, LinkedIn group, and Facebook page. What ideas bubble to the top of the stream in the month or week before the event? The messages that flow through, however hyped up on marketing juice, still represent topics people are paying attention to and paying to learn more about. Note who participates in the social media conversations. Reach out, respond, participate – you never know where it will lead.

## Quality Information

### Next Step: Get Ready to Research

Once you know *where* the editors and writers are, there's still work to be done to build a contact list. Visit the publication websites, find specific editorial contacts, and scrub the ones that don't cover the segments of the industry sandbox where you play.

The masthead is a quick source for researching the media sites you found in the trade show information. (BTW, if you don't have a PR background, you might not know that the masthead is where magazines list people like publishers, editors and contributing writers.)

Once you identify influencers and writers covering your target topics, follow them, comment on their work and build relationships first. Reach out to influencers to introduce yourself and find out what kinds of information will help them. Keep it low-key and don't be a pest. Build the relationship *before* you need something.

## The Influencer List

### List Maintenance Tips

Let's go back to that master list of media contacts: emails, names, publications, and areas of interest. If it seems like it takes a long time, then you're doing it right. It is very time-consuming, but in the long run, it's your best source for an affordable targeted press list.

### Routine Clean Upkeep

You will want to refine, update and add for the life of your list. I file bounced emails in a specific mail folder and go through them on a regular basis to clean up my list. Always be on the lookout for new contacts to add and bad contacts to fix.

### Organizing

Most people would tell you to use an Excel spreadsheet, and if that's what you're comfortable with, do so. Being a word geek, I usually use Word tables. Set up column headings like name, title, publication or website, email, phone and notes. If you are a spreadsheet person, you already know this, but put first names and last names in separate columns. Use the notes sections to cut and paste info about their interests and the publications like weekly/monthly/site/blogger, etc. This will save you lots of time later. Plus it will force you to know at least a little about each contact. Don't bother with faxes or snail mail addresses.

### The Opt Out Option

The first time you mail to your custom list, include an opt out statement, even if you have to manually update your list for the opters. Nothing wrong with that. Say something like "If you prefer not to receive information about XYZ, just let me know and I'll take you off the list." Simple, effective and it keeps you out of trouble.

### Use Descriptive Email Subject Lines

One organizing tip I'd like to share with you has to do with email. Say you've had a request for a photo from an editor, or a copy of a press release. When you send the information, think of the email subject line as the tab of a file folder (remember those?). Instead of a chipper, little non-descript subject line like, "Here's that information you needed," make the subject line simple and specific. For a photo, it might say, "COMPANY NAME photo of inkjet production printer" or "June 2010 COMPANY Z software launch press release."

When someone needs to find it again, they will stand a better chance of tracking it down. You'll save an editor time, and your photo won't get lost in an ever-swelling stack of email. I try to do this with every email I send, because I know how challenging it can be to go back and look for something I need when the subject line tells me nothing.

## Don't Forget the Analysts, or They'll Forget About You

### When the Analysts Come to Call

Industry analysts are another important subset of your influencer universe. Many companies have a dedicated analysts relations manager just to handle these sensitive relationships. A positive analyst report on your services or products is good as gold. B2B customers perceive analysts as highly credible. Companies sometimes bring in groups of analysts for a big annual briefing or to launch a new offering.

It's an important opportunity to spend face time with influencers and get out the message about why your company matters.

Here are some observations and tips that might help in case you've got a such a meeting coming up. Although this is about an analyst event, the tips could just as easily apply to a press gathering. Sometimes press and analysts are invited to the same meeting.

- Before you send out the first invitation, cross check against the industry's conference calendar. If there's another big industry event close to your date, don't schedule your gathering at the same time. You'll lose attendance. It's easier to change your date than for analysts to skip out on a major conference.
- Find a good corporate event planner and get out of her way. These people are a joy to watch, and they will take care of all the logistics, so you can take care of the content.
- Panels are a nice alternative to individual presentations, especially if you plan to showcase customers or let your execs take questions. Weak speakers won't be put on the spot, and the others can share the question/answer load. A good moderator can create some interesting dynamics that analysts will appreciate. You can give the panel a name and carry out the event theme.
- Give the analysts all your presentations. Why not? They are going to ask for them anyway, so be proactive. Put together a nice thumb drive with the slide decks, executive bios and photos, customer case studies (especially if these customers are speaking at the event for you.) white papers and reports on the key pillars of your messaging. You'll make the analysts' jobs easier, and you'll have more control over what they come away with.
- Don't start the agenda too early in the morning. It's going to be a long day. These analysts are on the road, coming to your turf, but they still have work to do, too. Start at 9 AM and give them some time to check email, return a few calls and enjoy a cup of coffee in peace. Maybe you'll have more of their attention later in the day if you give them time to take some things off their plate.

- Trust your company, your people and the analysts. Don't try to control every message and interaction. These are people coming to see people. They have a job to do. They aren't out to get you. Meet them halfway at least. You'll get better long-term results with honest interaction than too much structure.

## What Analysts Want to Hear

What do analysts want? I decided to ask one. Here are his remarks.

> *"It depends on their (the analysts') interests and clients. They primarily want to see that a company is different and has strong offerings that solve real problems that add value for customers. They want to connect with execs, professionally and personally, and feel free to call them as needed. (Like I know top people at companies who will take my calls, and I know many well enough to ask about kids, interests, etc.). That's the relationship stuff that takes time to build. And it builds trust, too."*

## Oooh, Scary

Here's where it might get scary for corporate marketers:

> *"At a big meeting, let the analysts ask tough questions and don't dodge the answers or blow smoke. They will figure out weaknesses anyway, and it's better to be up front about them, especially if you have a way forward to talk about."*

> *"No sales pitch. Talk about the industry and the business and how you have a strategy. And WHY you have the strategy you do."*

If you can't do that, you've just thrown one hell of a gathering, but you probably won't get much out of it in the long run.

## Your Influencer Relations Campaign

So you've identified your influencers and built your list. What do you want to tell them?

### Messaging and Content Strategy Tips:

- Focus on a few specific issues where your products and services can have a positive impact. What are your differentiators? Don't just guess. Ask product marketing and sales managers, and of course, senior executives.
- Frame discussions of issues in your company's terms, but offer useful, objective information and insights, not promotional or self-serving content.
- Leverage the power of storytelling when possible. Wrap the issues in stories. Give issues a context, a face. This makes the message more memorable. Start collecting stories from customers, sales and others.

### PR for Your Buyers

The Internet has forever changed PR and for the better. The audience is not just a handful of journalists anymore. Now your audience also includes millions of people with Internet connectivity and the ability to search. Of course, not all of those people will care about what you have to share, but your target buyers will.

Create releases that appeal directly to buyers' research needs, and then make it easy to find them. Write releases smartly populated with keyword-rich copy that aligns with the language of buyers. Include links to take readers to more content on your website and track them once they get there.

## Today's PR Target Audiences

- **Online influencers** who reach your target audience and who have potential to cover your customers' issues and industry topics. This could be trade press, bloggers and writers on media websites.

- **Business decision makers** who have potential need for your products or services.

### Own Your Distribution

Press releases that get placed online permanently expand your digital footprint. You don't have to wait for the media to pick up a release. You can take steps to get it planted online yourself.

Use a combination of these distribution methods:

- ✓ Press release distribution service
- ✓ Custom media list
- ✓ Post on website
- ✓ RSS news feed*
- ✓ Social sharing
- ✓ Social media posts
- ✓ Blogging

*Include the RSS feed opt in with your press release boilerplate (the standard "about" copy found at the end of every press release.) Do this with a link to your webpage where the reader can sign up for your RSS feed.

Press releases don't have to be traditional releases anymore. You can write them more as articles rather than straight news releases. Don't just send releases for "big news." Find reasons to send news to your influencers on a regular basis, such as:

- ✓ **Webinar pre and post releases** – First one plays up the issue the speaker will cover. Second one shares some informative nuggets and quotes from the presentation.
- ✓ **Conference speaker pre and post** – Same approach as webinar releases.
- ✓ **New white/"lite" paper available** – Make the release about the problem the white paper solves and the viewpoint of the author.
- ✓ **New blog** – Similar to above.
- ✓ **New SlideShare post** – Similar to other releases based on new content.
- ✓ **New research** – Especially research sponsored by your company.
- ✓ **New account signing** – Focus on the problem to be solved or outcome that's expected.
- ✓ **Use a mix of content** – Short form, issue-based, research, blogs, "lite" paper, executive summaries, articles.

## A Sample Plan

Here's a sample plan for influencer marketing that also hits the buyer's information needs.

### Month One: **Research and organize.**

- ✓ Research competitive PR and releases – For baseline, target media.
- ✓ Research target issues – Define and focus, angles, existing and needed content.

- ✓ Research and create assets you can pitch and promote in context of your key issues.
- ✓ Start your own editorial calendar for releases and pitches. Identify topics and schedule occasions for posting a release.
- ✓ Research external editorial calendars for rest of year. Find these in the Media Kit section of a publication's website. Add any relevant topics to your own editorial calendar for action.
- ✓ Research influencer information needs.
- ✓ Research media and influencer contacts.
- ✓ Craft and distribute two press releases.
- ✓ Build an approved customer reference list by topic. Journalists appreciate it when you can provide a good and willing source. They'll come to see you as someone who can help them.

Month Two: **Test the waters.**

- ✓ Two press releases.
- ✓ Pitch article.
- ✓ Start engagement with influencers.
- ✓ Ongoing development of contact list (this never ends).
- ✓ Write another blog.
- ✓ Continue with research work (this never ends).
- ✓ Write/ghostwrite, pitch, place articles, case studies.

PR is long-term. It takes discipline to stay on message and commitment to stay on course. Keep it simple. Build your program in layers and don't try to do it all at once. You can do a lot with a shoestring budget, but you do need a good head on your shoulders, a pleasant personality and half-decent writing skills.

# CHAPTER 5

## Marketing Toolkit – Press Releases

> *In this age of microblogging and two-second sound bites, almost no one has the attention span, or time, to read more than a few sentences.*
>
> — **Tim Frick,** Author, *Return on Engagement*

For a small business, medium-sized technology companies with limited marketing resources, or even big enterprises with lean staff, press releases can be your best friends. More affordable and versatile than advertising, you can send releases to clients, partners, employees and of course, the press and industry influencers like analysts, consultants and bloggers.

### Get It Out There

The best place to launch your press release is your own website. Then announce the link to your LinkedIn groups, Tweet it, and post it on your business Facebook page. Blog about it on your website. Tag it to your Delicious account, Google bookmarks or whatever bookmarking tool you use.

In addition to your own press list, use a free or next-to-it online press release service to get your releases posted online. However, if you frequently publish releases via a service that never get picked up, Google will see that as spam. Stick to meaningful releases.

## Grow Your Digital Footprint

The more frequently you send releases to your house list and seed them on the Internet, the bigger your digital footprint gets. And the more pervasive your online presence for your area of expertise, the easier it is for the right targets to find you using search.

Here's a recap of ideas to get you better acquainted with your new best friends – press releases:

- If you have no press list of your own, spend a little time and create a customized list.
- Always use an opt out offer in your email, whether it's an automated follow-up or something you handle yourself. Something like, "If you prefer not to receive information like this from XYZ Company, reply to sender with 'No Thanks' in the subject line."
- Write a simple email subject line – just state the news as succinctly as you can. Use a descriptive line that helps journos file and then relocate the info when they need it.
- Save the marketing speak and promotional fluff for the brochures. Journos and analysts don't fall for it, so it's not going to add anything to your branding here.
- Avoid the formula lead in: "XYZ Corp, an interplanetary leader in blah, blah, blah." Just get to the point of the news, or start out with an interesting narrative line or two that sets up the story.
- Figure out your keywords and use them in a natural way. Use one in your headline or subhead and in the first line of the release. Then scatter them throughout. Think of them as spices.
- Include links within your copy and try to link to a page that actually uses the terms you are linking from. Nothing is more aggravating than getting sent to a webpage that has nothing

to do with the original content. Word has a very simple tool for adding hyperlinks. Link to different pages within your website as appropriate.

- If you send an email that doesn't include the actual release, be sure you have an active link to the actual release. I've heard horror stories of PR "pros" who send an email without having the release ready to go.
- Have a contact person who is responsive and list their phone and email at the end of the release.
- Include graphics and photos when you can, or else offer to make these available upon request.

## How Do I Write a Press Release? That's a Good Question.

A strong press release can be the answer to a marketer's prayer, as long as you're praying for something fast, flexible, findable and affordable. But the question is, how do I write one? Even better, how do I write a good one? It all starts with good questions. If you plan strategic questions, your release will practically write itself. But powerful questions don't just help press releases. As a content marketer, you need the super power of good questions to create great content of any kind.

### Questions for Customer Success Stories

I have a menu of questions I use consistently to capture good, fresh press release content for news about customer successes. Editors are always receptive to news and stories about customers and end users. Since I mostly write about technology, both hardware and software, you'll find the questions will work well if that's your topic. Still, I've also applied these to other types of products and services, so you should find something you can use, no matter what you're writing about.

Some questions may sound redundant, and indeed, they are. I have found if you ask the same thing in slightly different ways, sometimes you get more elaboration on the answer. Or occasionally, a different answer. And if this list seems too long for one interview, you're right again. Don't plan to use every question. Pick the ones that seem most natural for your topic or customer or you.

So as to not overwhelm you completely, I'm going to share just some of my good questions. These first two categories deal with the key points of your press release.

## Problems and Opportunities

- Q What was the business problem or opportunity you needed to address?
- Q What business issues prompted you to get this technology?
- Q How did these problems impact your ability to serve customers and stay competitive?
- Q What product or technology did you use before?

## Business Impact and Benefits

- Q How does this new technology enhance your business strategy?
- Q What business problems does it solve and how?
- Q What applications and customers can you now better support?
- Q What business benefits do you expect from your investment?
- Q What market trends or issues does it address?
- Q What happens as a result of having the solution in place?
- Q What are you able to do differently or better, and what impact does this have on your business?

- Q How does this change affect the way you can position your company?
- Q Can you quantify your business results so far?
- Q Can you give examples of how the product has benefited your business?
- Q How has this technology changed the way you work?
- Q What results/benefits have you achieved?

Put together an interview based on a half dozen of these questions, and you'll come away with some decent information that really tells a good story.

### When Not to Write a Press Release

There are many good reasons for writing a press release, but here's one good reason not to – when you only plan to do just one. When your company commissions only one press release and then stops (cue the crickets,) bad things happen, like these:

- It looks like there's nothing going on at your company. What impression does it create to visit a website and see there's been no press release since 2009? Trust me, it looks lame.
- You create interest, and then drop the ball. The grail of press releases is to get editors and analysts to notice you, to recognize you. What makes you think that will happen with one measly release?
- You can't tell your story in one press release, can you? If you don't have more going on than one press release worth of news, what kind of story do you have?
- It's a waste of your money. You need more than a single release to build up presence and impact. If you don't plan to commit to a steady schedule of releases, save your money.
- You don't get better at it. It takes practice and just doing it

to develop your company voice. Talk, talk, talk to the marketplace.

- Your digital footprint remains no more than a digital toe print. Your customers and prospects are looking for companies like yours, and they are looking online. Put a steady flow of press releases out there and help them find you and understand you.

### Carry on a Conversation

Let me put it another way, or several. When you only publish one press release every twelve months or so, it's like building a brick wall, but only laying the first course of bricks. It's starting a conversation, and never saying anything beyond the first sentence. It's striking a match for a publicity bonfire and then letting the fire go out.

### Once Is Not Enough. Nor Is Twice.

If I've said it once, I've said it a thousand times: of all the marketing tactics, press release writing gives the most return on investment. But you've got to do it - often - and do it well. You can pay a pro to write press releases piecemeal, but secretly, your writer is shaking her head in puzzlement. Why, why, why? Yes, releases cost money to do professionally, but hello, since when was good marketing talent free? How much would you expect to spend on one print ad, if you still truck with that marketing dinosaur? One ad will buy you the equivalent of a whole campaign of releases.

## Get the Headline and First Paragraph Right

### No Lawyers Needed

Someone once asked me what is the law about the lead sentence in a press release? *"There aren't any laws about press releases,"*

I replied, restraining a smug chuckle. *"It's whatever your company wants it to be."*

Let me be clear: there are no rules about writing press releases. There are rules for the words you use in filing SEC materials. There are guidelines for the disclaimer sheets for every prescription drug we take. But press releases? It's mostly been tradition and what you learned in college, along with some common sense, like including the date, for instance. Kinda need to know that, but things like location don't seem to matter much now, when most press releases get distributed online. Your dateline could be Mars; it won't make any difference. (But wouldn't that be news!)

## Time to Break Some Rules

In my career, I've written hundreds of releases, and I suggest it's time to break a few rules and create some new ones. Let's start with this truth: The headline and first paragraph are the most important elements of your press release. The headline is a traditional element, but it's got an important role.

The jobs of the headline, subhead and first paragraph are to:

- Capture editors' and readers' interest
- Contribute to search optimization
- Provide a snapshot of your news
- Set the tone of the news

## Write Your Headline Last

A helpful hint for almost any kind of copy project that involves a headline is to write the headline last. Otherwise, you waste a lot of time picking over every word, and it probably won't be that solid. Write the lead paragraph first, then let the headline evolve out of that. Think of the headline as a summary of the lead paragraph. Strip it of every extra word, like "the," "Inc.," and

"and." Use the streamlined headlines you see in newspapers and magazines as your model.

**Please Retire this Old Line**

I'm going to jump right in now with one of my biggest peeves about press releases. Do your recognize this formula? "TechnologyTreats, Inc., a global leader in quality solutions that delight customers, announced today..." Everyone is a global leader. All chiefs, no Indians.

I don't know why companies continue to lead off with releases this way. It's so boring and so wrong. If the first 250 words are the most important, why are you wasting space on such a tired, old line? If that's the first line on every release you ever send out (and believe me, for many companies, it is) sooner or later, important eyeballs will start skimming over your news and missing what's important.

**Think of It as Writing an Article**

The foundation of your B2B press release should be the intriguing opening paragraph. Think of it as the beginning of a news article, which is what it hopefully will be. Editors in trade journals and other B2B media are likely to run the release as is, if it sounds like something they would write themselves. Here's an example.

> *September 9, 2014 – As the managed print services (MPS) market explodes, so has the body of research, webinars, newsletters, journals and other content created about it. Just one year ago, BrainTrust Group launched the PlanetMPS.com website to bring the latest trends, ideas and best practices to MPS practitioners and end users. Now, on the anniversary of that introduction, BrainTrust has launched an expanded version of that site in MPSuniverse.com. The new content-centric community organizes a wealth of multi-media resources in one place for the MPS*

*community, including immediate online access to the latest industry blogs. An experienced team will curate the material, adding new content and keeping information in all formats accessible and up to date.*

This paragraph reads like the beginning of an article. Adding quotes and anecdotes will flow naturally from this start, and make the piece more interesting and readable to its target audience. It could also stand alone as a complete piece.

## Key in on Keywords

*"Use the words that matter most to your customers in titles, links and body copy to inform and inspire them to take action. Text used in titles should make it easy for readers to understand the topic of the page quickly, in the first few words."*

— **Lee Odden,** Toprank Online Marketing blog

I love this advice. It's simple, practical and wise. The SEO backlash advocates not writing for search engines, but for the specific people who might search for what you have to offer. Figure out what keywords and phrases would lead a seeker to your information and include a selective mix of a few in the lead paragraph. Put a strong keyword in the headline and one in the subhead, too. But the most important thing to remember is, write good content that people will find useful.

## Create a Standalone Story

One sign that your headline and lead paragraph are done well is if you can jettison the rest of the release and tell the story with just those pieces, as we did with the example above. You never know what will happen to that release once you send it out into the world to fend for itself. Think of how much of a release actually gets presented when Google returns a set of search results. What if a news feed presents just the headline and first sentence or two of its stream of releases? Do you want the reader to see a generic corporate lead in, or would it be better to give them a sense of the story right away? Information overload has most readers skimming everything anyway. Better to get their attention quickly before they move on.

### Who, What, When, Where and Why Not

Just as the headline and paragraph are primary elements, the information in them also has a hierarchy. For today's skeptical journalists, time-strapped editors and skimming readers, forget who, what, when and where. What matters in a B2B press release are two things – what and why, especially the why. The rest is secondary. If you can convince the editorial gatekeeper why the news matters, why it is an important announcement for your market segment, why anyone in your industry should care, the rest of the W's will follow along nicely.

Tell the news and then tell why it matters to the audience served by the media you send it to. That's it. If you can't tell why it matters, why are you doing a release?

## Writing a B2B Press Release Quote? Don't Get Excited.

Depending on whom you listen to, the press release is either totally dead, fully digital or hopelessly dated. Without question, press releases have changed dramatically. The days of snail mailing and faxing releases are long, LONG gone. Most releases probably don't even get printed as hardcopies. Because we can, we pack releases with key words, links, video and images. We don't write them just for gatekeeping editors anymore. Anyone using a search engine can find your posted release.

Some changes are for the better; others strike me as a confusing waste of time. But one thing that hasn't changed is the use of quotes in a B2B press release. In some contemporary releases, the quotes are given their own special section, complete with a clever title such as "Executive Quotes." (Like no one could otherwise find the quotes in a two-page document?)

## Readers Are People, So Sound Like a Human Being

Quotes show the human side of your company. Too bad so many press release quotes don't sound like anything a human being would actually say.

> *"We are excited about this unique opportunity to bring leading edge solutions to customers in these dynamic markets," said Bland Suitguy, Vice President of Vagueness, Inc. "We will focus on best-in-breed quality on a going forward basis."*

What a wasted opportunity to say something meaningful. (Of course, you know I totally made that one up, but tell the truth, you've read lots of quotes just like that, haven't you?)

Like the example above, the typical B2B press release quote is more a self-serving homage to the company putting out the release, than something intended to be of actual interest to a reader. It's written that way because it's always been done that way. Let's all agree not to do that anymore, okay? And let's especially agree not to admit "We are excited" in our press releases. Pinky promise?

## It's Up to You – Don't Encourage Lameness

Think about quotes from the perspective of the editor on the receiving end who controls the posting of your release. Editors have to fill a magazine or a website with content, and have no time to spend making all the releases they get sound pretty or smarter. When you take the time to craft an intelligent quote, editors get article-quality content without having to write it themselves – or pay for someone else to do it. Sure, editors will run releases with lame or bland quotes. They do all the time, but that still doesn't make it a good quote.

### Be a Good Journalist

A good quote raises the journalistic value of your release and improves its appeal to an editor. It makes your company sound smart, not bland. Why not use the opportunity to have someone say something that makes your executives sound visionary and demonstrates their thought leadership?

### Write the Quote You'd Like to See

In the B2B world, press release quotes come from:

- Your company spokesperson, who should to be director level or above, not the PR person
- Clients who have some connection to your announcement
- Industry analysts and gurus who can put your news in context or validate your positioning
- Business partners and collaborators who may be a part of the announcement

In reality, most B2B press release quotes are manufactured for these executives who "speak" them. "Write the quote you'd like to see," recommends one marketing veteran. "The client will often use it or just modify slightly, so give it your best shot and use your own judgment."

### Ten Tips for Quote Writers

What's the point of the press release quote? If a release doesn't have one, does anyone notice? Maybe not, but why not take advantage of this special section of your release? Use your quote "real estate" strategically. It's a chance for the company to speak. Consider these ideas as you plan your next press release quote:

- Quotes can be opinions, so if you need to sneak one into a release, that's the place to do it.

- Work in something specific about why this announcement makes you better than the competition.
- Frame the announcement in context of your bigger corporate strategy.
- Weave in a key word or search phrase that just couldn't fit in anywhere else.
- Point out industry trends that are relevant to the news.
- Make an emotional connection that isn't suited to the otherwise factual nature of the rest of the release, but don't say you're happy/thrilled/excited or some other high school gush.
- Describe an example of how the news solves problems for your customers. Tell a little story.
- Talk about why your company felt this was an important step to take. Be specific and honest.
- Use "According to" to vary from "he/she said," especially if there are multiple quotes in the release.
- Keep quotes short and to the point. Avoid multiple-paragraph quotes. We don't like wordy people, so no wordy quotes, please.

### Too Many Good Quotes? Quote Gallery!

Most B2B quotes are created by a PR person, but what if you actually conduct an interview to capture comments for your press release? And what if the result is a hodge podge of interesting but disjointed comments? Don't despair. Turn them into a "quote gallery" organized by topical subheads that a trade journal editor can pull from at will. It's an approach well suited to the bite-size info needs of the online world.

## Publish as an Interview

Instead a single quote, if you have a lot of good copy to work from, turn the press release into an interview with the person who's being quoted. This makes the release a little different from the run-of-the-mill release. Just be sure the final quote-driven product is professional, focused on your release topic and something an editor can use as a standalone piece without embarrassment.

## Keep It Real As You Make It Up

Make it real. Think conversation. What would your CEO tell an editor – or customer – about this news if they were sitting face to face over a cup of coffee or glass of beer? Make the quote sound like something a real person would actually say. Read it out loud to see if it sounds real.

## Be Real Bold

Most executives are reluctant to "say" anything provocative or contrarian, and I can understand that. But a juicy, provocative quote, within limits, can drive more attention to your release. Take a risk. Be bold with your quote.

## Some Samples

For fun, here are a few random but actual quotes from B2B press releases. See if they do anything for you. And for transparency purposes, I did write one of these.

> *"For channel partners, we look for ISVs with customers generating contracts, renewals and invoices in vertical markets like insurance, government and banking. Integrating our software into their solution saves ISVs time and money. Instead of developing and maintaining their own document creation tool, they can almost immediately bring this functionality to customers through our software," said XYZ Software CEO, John Doe.*

*Looking forward to his new role, Williams said, "I am excited to bring my experience and knowledge to the team. I have never seen a product in this market that brings so much to the table in terms of functionality. JazzyJazz is an incredibly powerful tool that simplifies the entire workflow with a true turnkey solution from production to delivery to payment receipt."*

*Blankety Food Service has acquired Yummies, a leading broadline foodservice distributor based in St. Louis, MI. Joe Snack, chief executive officer of Blankety Food Service, said, "Yummies is a great company with a strong family heritage. Their dedication to high-quality service is an ideal fit with Blankety Food Service's culture and commitment to exceptional customer service."*

**No Such Thing as Rules**

There's no rule that says you only send releases just for "big news." With a little thought, you can find good reasons to send bits of news all the time. Releases don't have to be long, and in fact, they shouldn't be. They do have to be interesting and topical. Think like an editor. Think like a customer. What would interest them?

I have written many a press release, and I still think the concept is valid, even in a social marketing strategy. We may need to agree on a new name for this tool, but we still need to send regular, useful strategic content to a group of influencers. Just try running a marketing strategy without it. Indeed, the "new" press release in its many forms fuels many a blog and article.

What shouldn't change is this: Does this tell my audience something useful? Does it communicate something that moves the needle on our positioning? Does it persuade the reader to keep us on their short list? It's all still about persuading and selling.

# CHAPTER 6

## Marketing Toolkit – Case Studies

> *Find interesting stories to tell – look to your customers or challenges in your industry. Don't worry so much about talking about your products. Build an audience first with compelling stories.*
>
> — **Tim Washer,** "Corporate Comedian", *Cisco*

Case studies rank with the most powerful and useful content marketing tools you can have in your bag of tricks. You can clearly and in (reasonable) detail tell the story of how you helped a real customer solve problems. The market sees the stories as credible endorsements. (Just don't use that word anywhere in your pitch to the potential customer. Too scary.) But there's just one problem.

### THE PROBLEM WITH CUSTOMER CASE STUDIES? THE CUSTOMERS!

#### Problem #1

The biggest problem with writing good B2B case studies? The customers, of course!

Some customers are thrilled with the idea of seeing their company and people recognized in an article. Others react as though you've asked them to out every skeleton in their corporate closet. Or your contact in Operations does agree to participate, but Marketing or Legal cancels the project before it gets started, or worse yet, after you've written the damn thing. Or they won't agree to let you use their company by name. Sometimes companies can take weeks or even months to get your copy through their internal reviews. Or the contact you started with ends up leaving the company before the project is finished, and you have to start all over. Yes, those darn customers.

### Problem #2

The second biggest problem with writing good B2B case studies? NOT writing them.

Now, the problems described above don't happen all the time, but they are common enough to make it difficult to regularly move a good case study all the way from beginning interview to final review. For that reason, you should try to have multiple case studies in process simultaneously. Hopefully that way, you may get one done every month if you're VERY lucky. And one a month would be a wonderful thing for your content marketing efforts.

**How can you make case studies a positive experience for you and your customers?**

### A Dozen Ways to Ensure Case Study Success

Don't give up just because a few customers throw the occasional obstacle in front of you. You're a tough marketeer, and you now have a dozen ways to improve your chances of getting a good customer case study to market.

1. Include a commitment to participate in case studies (and press releases) in your sales agreements.
2. Pitch the value to the customer of using the case study for their own marketing purposes.
3. Make them aware that they will also benefit from this professionally developed marketing tool — and at no cost.

4. Recognize that they are busy and explain that demands on their time will be kept to a minimum.
5. Provide your interview questions in advance, so customers can prepare with confidence.
6. Proactively acknowledge the need to work with their marketing or legal people during reviews.
7. Enlist the customer's account manager to pitch the story on your behalf. Leverage the good relationships your sales people have with their clients.
8. Make it clear in advance how and where the case study content will be used.
9. Try to get their agreement to use the story for other purposes such as a press release. Even if they won't, they may feel obligated to throw you a bone and be more cooperative on the case study.
10. Give them a deadline for having their reviews completed.
11. Offer the choice of a phone interview or email responses to gather background.
12. Get everything in writing or in an email – participation agreements, reviews, revisions, approvals.

Before anyone gets the wrong idea, I really do love talking to customers. Participating in a case study interview makes me very proud of the companies who hire me to write for them. And the smart business people who are the subjects of these pieces are impressive as hell. It's stimulating to hear success stories from the "real world" and to help give some recognition to everyone's hard work.

## When Customers Say NO to Case Studies

Case studies can be your most useful tools for building credibility with prospects, editors, analysts and other influencers. Case studies help your sales team convince buyers to sign. They can be repurposed extensively in print and on line.

The down side – case studies are some of the most difficult marketing opportunities to capture. For various reasons, companies are often reluctant to participate. Do you ever struggle with unenthusiastic customers who would make great stories? Here are some ideas to help you get testimonial-averse customers to join in.

- Pitch the value of the PR they will also receive from the project.
- Offer the completed case study for them to use in their own marketing or website.
- Remind them they will get a professionally written marketing tool at no cost.
- Explain the steps in the case study process up front, such as interview, review, revisions, final draft.
- Commit to keeping their time investment to a minimum.
- Offer to provide questions in advance, so customer will be comfortable with what you want to write and line up any other people they want to join in the interview.
- Offer to work closely with their marketing and legal reviewers.
- Offer to write the story making the company anonymous, such as "a leading financial services provider" instead of Bank of Whatever.

It's a shame to let good customer stories go untold. What techniques have you used to get customers to participate?

# Step-by-Step Guide: Writing Effective B2B Case Studies

## Step 1: Gathering Useful Background Material

Case studies, testimonials, success stories — whatever you call them, your company should be cranking some out on a regular basis. Editors love customer case studies. Sales people love case studies. Even customers love customer case studies. They can make everyone look good.

This guide takes you through the case study creation process step by step. You'll see why these steps can save you time and add depth to your story.

### Formula or No Formula

Over the years, quite a few clients of mine have requested their case studies to be in some version of a problem / challenge / solution / benefit formula. Of course, I do what my clients want, but my preference is to let the case study take its own shape. I think it results in a more readable, interesting story and can still include all the typical elements. Just because it's a case study doesn't mean it has to be boring!

The reason I bring this structural point up during the background gathering stage is, for me anyway, the structure of the story emerges out of the information you gather, not the other way around. If you prefer to use the formula approach because of company policy, template constraints or whatever, these background ideas will still be useful.

One thing to note: If a case study is to be pitched to an editor and your company uses the formula approach, consider writing another version of the case study that is told in more of a journalistic or narrative style. Editors aren't going to get excited about a formula-based case study that they have to rework to use.

## Talk to Sales First

First, before you write anything, talk to the sales account manager about the customer. Make sure the project has actually been cleared through the customer and their marketing department, if necessary. There's nothing sadder than writing a great case study, only to find out you can't use it.

Things to ask the sales account manager:

- What does she think are the most important points of the story?
- What things should you as the writer make sure to ask the customer about?
- Can she explain the background, problem and solution in the customer's terms?
- Find out if there were any "issues" and if any are still unresolved.
- Find out if the sales manager prefers to make the first customer contact about the interview, or if they are comfortable with you doing it.
- Does she want to be on the interview call?

## Are They Really Ready Yet?

Make sure the customer has enough experience in using the product to make a case study out of the story. If it's a new installation, you're better off writing a press release at this point, and revisiting the account in six months or so, after they've had time to build up some experience and results with it.

## Research the Customer Company Online

Go to the company website to get a feel for their business and markets. See if there is any boilerplate description about their business niche and unique value proposition. These will be good points to weave into the story, and there's a practical side, too.

You won't have to spend as much time on the company background in the live interview, and much of the background copy will be practically pre-approved by the customer, because you took it straight from their website.

Do this and present the company in a favorable, progressive light, and that will accelerate the review process. (Trust me, you'll probably need every speed trick you can muster. Reviews and approvals can literally take months.) The website may also prompt ideas to help you frame your questions more specifically and customize the interview.

Once you've gathered your background material, you're ready to set up a call with your customer.

## STEP 2: Setting Up for the Interview

Every B2B marketer needs a good library of case studies. Your sales people love them. Editors love them, and so do most customers. So, you've done your research and gathered all your background materials. Now you're ready to move ahead with an interview — or two.

### Your First Contact with the Customer

Once you have the go ahead to do a case study, reach out to the customer by phone or email first, and copy your sales account manager. (Sometimes your sales people will want to sit in on the interview, and that's okay.) In your first outreach, explain the interview, draft and review processes and give the customer an idea of the time frame involved. Promise to send the interview questions in advance, and do that. This raises their comfort level immensely. It also helps you structure your interview and story later. Plus, the customer will know if they need to bring in reinforcements to answer the questions.

### A Live One

You can offer to let the customer send responses via email if that's more convenient, and then have a phone call later if necessary to fill in any gaps. A live interview is better though, because you'll often uncover some gems you hadn't expected, or you can ask impromptu questions that come up during the call. And here's something odd, but true. I find the most valuable nuggets of the interview often come in the last five or ten minutes of the call. Maybe the customer has relaxed, or maybe you've just drilled down to the good stuff by then. The point is, conserve your mental energy and stay alert until the very end.

### To Record or Not to Record

Some writer friends swear by recording interviews for customer testimonials. I can't recommend any good ways to do this because I never record interviews. I'm an extremely fast typist, so I whiz along capturing comments on my keyboard. Because the notes are just for me, I don't worry about typos. Plus I don't have the time to listen to the interview again. If my questions are good, I can almost rough out the story as I go. Of course, if you do prefer to record, let the customer know and get their approval.

### Pictures Anyone?

At some point, you'll want some pictures to go with the case study. Graphic designers are good at finding stock photos, but the real deal images are always best. However, they must be of good quality for editors to want them. There are several ways to get pictures to go with your case study. Ask the client to take some for you. See if your account manager can swing by with a camera. Ask for hi-res digital images in tif, eps or jpeg formats. Get people shots, head shots, headquarters shots – whatever you can. If something is produced using your company's product, for example, software used to generate a personalized direct mail piece, try to get a picture or two of sample output pieces.

A friend used to hire local photographers at reasonable prices by contacting the photography department of the newspaper in the city where the customer was located. Newspaper photojournalists don't make huge salaries, so you might get a qualified person for a good rate. They also know the area and can find your client's location. Plus they know how to get in, get the picture and get out quickly. If you start early enough, you'll have time to track down photos using any of these methods.

### About the Review Process

By far, the longest stage of the case study process is not the writing, but the reviewing. It can go on and on and on. I've had some reviews take months to get through customers' internal approval channels. Sometimes your key contact will leave the company before the review is complete. It can be a pain. About all you can do is stay on it, and stay in touch. The one tip I can share is, when you send a reminder email about a case study review, the use of an all-caps "SECOND REQUEST" in the email subject line for some reason seems to work when all else fails.

And don't forget this little detail. As you go through reviews and sign offs, and as you collect photos to use in the layout, do get some form of approval documentation. Google for release forms, or make your own. Ask your legal department for help. For some companies, a simple email approving use of a piece is enough. Just do something to CYA.

## STEP 3: Plan Your Interview

### Good Questions. Good Interview. Good Case Study.

If you've been following along, you're probably ready to gather the raw material for your case study in the customer interview. It's important to think strategically about your queries, because you can structure your article around them as you go. Good questions lead to good interviews which lead to good case studies. Structure the interview with your story in mind. Do it right, and the content will be organized automatically as you conduct the interview. The questions you ask will determine what kind of information you collect.

### Keep It to a Dozen Questions

Try to keep your list of questions to about a dozen. Too many questions will intimidate the customer or give them the idea that it will be just too much work to participate. **Plan your questions carefully.** You don't want to go back to the customer later with a lame-o request for something you should have known to ask about the first time. (It's okay and somewhat expected to have a few follow-up questions as you work on your draft.) Remember, to save time and ensure accuracy, get the customer's company background from their website.

### Build a Question File

To help things go faster, I keep a digital file of interview questions (my "Fragen File") that I can customize for different clients or subjects. I've developed the list of questions over many years of writing and interviewing.

Many of case studies I write and hence the questions I use are geared to B2B technology customers. However, I find some questions are just universal, especially those about business goals, problems and outcomes. For example, these can apply to almost any industry:

- Q Tell me about your customers and markets.
- Q What kinds of problems did you have before you implemented this solution from company X?
- Q What feedback have you had from your clients and your internal users?

As I do more writing about a particular company, technology or industry, I usually build up a subset of questions specific to that topic. Having a question file to draw on will make your interview preparation go faster, and you will be less likely to forget something important. Avoid asking yes/no questions because those answers won't make much of a story. Make each one an open-ended question.

## Some B2B Interview Questions

Here are some starter questions for you to build your own question database. I encourage you to customize them for your clients and markets. Note that most of the questions try to probe connections between the solution and its impact on the customer's business. You might want multiple versions of the same question to see if you get different responses.

- Q Name and title of person to be quoted (Get this out of the way first.)
- Q What/How many [hardware systems/software modules/service plans] were purchased? Where will they be installed and when? (Another basic one to get out of the way early on.)
- Q What were your main business/operational reasons for selecting the system/product/software?
- Q In your opinion, what are some of most significant features of the product and how do they benefit you?
- Q Tell me about how the system supports your company's "green" initiatives. Why is this important to you?
- Q Will the systems replace existing equipment? How will this be an advantage?
- Q What problems can you now solve or what opportunities can you pursue with the solution?
- Q How will the investment change or enhance your business capabilities? How does it give you a competitive advantage? How will this impact the quality of your services?
- Q What does the solution enable you to do differently or better?

- Q What impact does this have on your business?
- Q How does the technology support your business strategy?
- Q Any other thoughts? (This is a good wrap up question for getting that last bit of good content out of the interview.)
- Q Can you provide any high res pictures (300 dpi TIF images are good) of your production area, applications, people to be quoted, company HQ, etc.

You don't want to use all of these at one time. Remember, keep it to 12 questions or less. I do recommend numbering your list, rather than bulleting. As you write up the responses, number them so you can more easily match them up to their question.

### Organize Questions into Categories

Sometimes I group questions by categories, such as "About your market" or "About your operations and workflow." Because people get intimidated by a long set of questions, grouping makes the process a little less scary. Three questions on each of four topics are less worrisome than one big list of 12 questions. The interview structure looks more organized as well, and the interviewee can better understand what you are trying to do. Grouping can also guide the framework or outline for your article.

### B2B Case Study Question Categories

- Company background
- Selection criteria
- About the customer's operation
- Business problem or opportunity
- Business results

### Bringing in Reinforcements

The typical interview customer in my world is going to be an IT or operations executive, and occasionally someone from the C-suite. Sometimes a customer will decide to include other departments in the interview after they've seen what I plan to ask — another good reason for sending questions in advance. It's not uncommon to bring in their operations or production manager or a marketing person, once they know what might come up. That's usually a good thing, too, because they will play off one another, and you get more perspectives on the topic.

Clients like to feel prepared, especially for an interview. When they see thoughtful, well-organized questions, they can see you are serious, and that you know what you are doing. My favorite all-time answer is when someone thoughtfully says, *"That's a good question."* Then I know I've done a good job thinking about the interview and the story.

# CHAPTER 7

## Marketing Toolkit – White Papers

> *Focus on the core problem your business solves and put out lots of content and enthusiasm, and ideas about how to solve that problem.*
>
> — **Laura Fitton,** Inbound Marketing Evangelist, *HubSpot*

White papers and their fancy, digital hipster cousins - *eBooks* - are like the Clydesdales of your marketing content. (Hipster Clydesdales?) They can pull a big load.

### WHATCHA GONNA DO WITH THAT WHITE PAPER?

#### PART 1 - Marketing White Papers – with More Writing

Let's look at those content heavyweights: white papers (and whenever you see white paper, automatically assume eBook as well.) Let's say you've just finished one, and you're pretty darn proud of it. While you still have your writer around, don't stop with the white paper. The dumbest thing you can do is to take that creation and let it languish on your website. Repurpose, reuse, recycle – what works for the planet works for your white paper.

Here are some ideas to maximize that content investment:

- Of course, do a **press release** on your latest white paper. Tell why it's important and to whom and then where to get it. The point is to position your company as a thought leader. Make the link to the white paper registration the call to action.

Quote factoids from the white paper. Use quotes from some of the white paper sources. This release will write itself.

- For the foreseeable future, include this white paper in your **industry conference press kits**. Press kits aren't just for press releases.
- And speaking of press releases – aren't we always? – add the white paper to your corporate **boilerplate**, the "About" stuff at the end. Something like, "XYX Company offers a free white paper to help [target audience here] better understand and leverage the trends and challenges facing their industry." Call me if you want something a little snappier and more specific.
- **Blog** about it with a link to the download. Even better, get someone else to blog about it. And someone else, and someone else...
- Spin off an **article** and have the download as the call to action. You can pitch the article to a trade pub.

## PUT THAT WHITE PAPER TO WORK

### PART 2 - Marketing White Papers Socially

Part 1 focused on ideas to promote your white paper using written techniques. Now in Part 2, when I say "market your white paper socially," I'm talking about ways that involve either human delivery or through a social channel.

### White Paper Webinar

Make the white paper topic the focus of a webinar. And if you are already a "webinarista," well, get busy. It's a little online debut party, so invite your database, talk about the white paper topic, then invite attendees to visit the link and get their own copy. Your primary content sources may be the best presenters, and they might appreciate the additional exposure. Of course, you'll also need another press release to promote your webinar.

### Socialize It

Tweet it, Link it, Facebook it. You don't have to say much, just something like: "The latest white paper from [company] is a must read for IT execs who struggle with [topic here]. Find it here – LINK." The length will need some tweaking for copy-anorexic Twitter, and use bitly.com to shrink and track the URL.

### Market by Email

Promote your white paper to your database via email marketing. It's a good reason to reach out, and it reinforces your thought leadership. Make the white paper download the call to action. Or call it the bonus gift for placing an order, signing up for an online community or registering for a conference.

### Get Some Help

Investigate online pubs, portals and PDF search sites that offer white papers to readers. Many of the technology-focused websites do this, but most aren't free. If you have a strong white paper that showcases your expertise, the expense might be worth it. These sites typically have a lead service tied in with their white paper programs, so it's not a passive posting.

### White Papers for Presentations

Presentations and white papers go hand in hand. Scour around for conferences that are at least a few months out or more, and pitch a presentation based on your white paper topic. You or your writer should have no trouble creating a presentation based on the white paper. Use the white paper itself – or a link – as the handout.

### Post It

Post it to your website, but just remember, search engines sometimes have trouble with PDF files. Include a text summary of the white paper using alluring keywords, so the search spiders can find your document more easily.

Every once in a while, someone will say "no one reads white papers anymore." It's all about videos or infographics or something else quick and easy to view. Every piece of marketing content has its place, and there's still a place for white papers, especially in B2B selling. The products and services we offer usually can't be explained in a two-minute video or a static graphic. When buyers are in the research stage, which is up to 70 percent of the buying cycle now, they want information. This is the role of the white paper. Make yours something that helps a customer understand what they need to solve a problem and what the current thinking is about it.

That said, most people don't want to read 20 pages on anything but reading for pleasure. Do think about a manageable document, maybe not even calling it a white paper, but perhaps an executive summary or even a "lite" paper. Keep it informative and well written, and your long format content will still have a place in your toolkit.

# CHAPTER 8
## Marketing Toolkit – The Pitch

*“Pitching articles is an art. You must know your publication, its audience, and most importantly, your editor or reporter.”*

— **Lyn Chamberlin,** Vice President for Marketing and Communications, *Sarah Lawrence College*

### How to Write an Article Pitch for Trade Journals

**Ready?**

Through a couple of examples, I hope to give you some ideas about how to sell an editor on your article idea as well as on your article's author as a topic expert.

What follows is an emailed pitch I wrote a few years ago. (The names are changed so I don't have to bother with permission from anyone.) The target publication covers digital printing, and I researched their editorial calendar to discover an upcoming feature was planned on sustainability in printing. This pitch is longer than most I write, but there were a number of angles to propose. Notice that it gets right to the point.

**Example #1 — Help the Editor Visualize the Article**

> *Hi [editor],*
>
> *As you prepare your March article on sustainability in production printing, have you thought about exploring any of these points?*

- *The chain of custody at every stage of a document's lifecycle, from materials and energy sources to processes and practices. What points can the print room influence and control?*
- *Paper is an infinitely renewable resource, but the Green Press Initiative reports that paper accounts for 40 percent of the waste stream, and the paper industry emits the fourth-highest CO levels among all manufacturers. What efforts are being made to make paper used in digital printing more green?*
- *Reducing overproduction is a key recommendation of the Environmental Trends and Climate Impacts Report. How does digital printing offer a "kinder, gentler" way to print?*
- *As more technology vendors jump on the green bandwagon, the challenge becomes identifying sustainable business partners. Does a provider conduct business in an environmentally responsible manner? Can he offer evidence of sustainable business practices or help produce a chain of custody?*
- *Waste handling and emissions are top-of-mind concerns. Reducing ozone emissions should be a key initiative for any eco-responsible company. What does this mean for inplant print operations?*

*If any of these ideas are of interest, you or your writer may want to speak with the experts at BigPrinterManufacturer, Inc. BPM has a long tradition of sustainable business practices, and has been working with commercial printing customers to support their "green" initiatives. I can connect you with BPM experts who can talk to the sustainability issues and solutions relevant to your print room audience. Let me know if you'd like to do that, and thanks for your consideration.*

*Regards,*

### What to Note about this Pitch

I think there are several things to note about this pitch:

- It references an article topic that is already scheduled in the publication's editorial calendar.
- It uses reports and studies to make a point. This shows the editor I have information to share that's not tied up in corporate marketing BS.
- I suggest at least five different angles that might suit the planned article
- Through leading questions, I set up some ideas for a writer to explore in the article.
- I offer subject matter experts from BigPrinterManufacturer to supplement the studies and other information.

### Example #2 — Position Your Author As Expert

Often when I make a pitch on behalf of a client, I focus on the expertise of the proposed author as an inducement to consider the article idea. It might go like this:

**Email subject:**

Article proposal — *Outsourcing document development: Best practice or poor choice?*

**Email copy:**

*Dear [editor's name]*

*The topic of outsourcing document development usually generates controversy and misinformation. Does outsourcing make economic sense for companies that lack that expertise, or does it put them at the mercy of an outside provider? That's precisely why accurate, insightful analysis of the issue is so important to your readers who deal with this problem on a daily basis.*

*With this in mind, what would be your interest in an article that looks at both sides of the controversy and helps your readers make the best choices for their businesses? Ellen Smith, vice president of technology at Documents, Inc., has over 16 years of experience in all areas of document development. She speaks regularly at industry events, and is a frequent contributor to respected blogs and publications.*

*If this might be valuable for your readers, we can provide an outline for an 800-1,000 word article written by Ellen that looks at these topics:*

- *What are the risks of do-it-yourself document development?*
- *How do you measure the skill and quality of an outside developer?*
- *What do best practices in document development look like?*

*We understand your publication won't accept articles that are promotional in nature, and we promise to provide a professionally written piece with useful information for your readers. Let me know if you'd like more information or if you'd like to get something started. You can reach me at...(and so on.)*

**Things to Note about the Second Pitch Example**

- It leads with an intriguing email subject line.
- It sets up an interesting problem that is topical and trendy for this market.

- It establishes the expertise of your author.
- It describes the scope of the proposed article, even to the word count.
- It acknowledges that promotional pieces aren't acceptable.
- It continually references the needs of the reader.

### Should You Follow Up?

These two samples should give you a feel for the types of things to include in an article pitch to a trade journal. If you're successful, you could end up snagging the assignment for your company expert (which you may in turn help ghostwrite.) Or if the editor assigns the story to a staff writer or a freelancer, hopefully she will include your company on the suggested contact list provided to the writer.

Here's an important tip, though. Don't get too pushy about following up with the editor regarding your pitch. It's just bad PR form. At the most, you might drop a short note reminding them about the pitch and asking if there was any interest. If you don't get any response, take your idea and move on to another publication with it.

### Get in the Game

Don't be intimidated by pitching. Be sincere, be prepared and be relevant. It's a numbers game. The more ideas you suggest, the better your chances of having one accepted. Get out there and get in the game.

HELP AN EDITOR. PITCH A GOOD STORY.

### Editorial Pitches to Trade Journals

Do an editor a favor. Bring them a great story idea and a good plan to get it written. Here are more suggestions on where to find ideas that will make an editor smile and win you some strategic coverage.

## What You Can Learn from a Website

Because there is so much information available online, you have no excuse for not taking advantage of it to find ideas for an editorial pitch. If you haven't already, explore the website of the publication you want to target. As you read through every nook and cranny, keep notes. You're brainstorming, you're mind mapping, baby!

While you're there, get the media kit, and if the site offers a Business of Performing Audits or BPA report (an independent validation of their circulation,) you can research the publication's readership. BPA Worldwide audits the circulation of business-to-business and consumer magazines. You'll find details about reader titles and market breakdowns. This will give you clues about crafting and positioning your pitch. You can also do a reality check to see if is really the right audience for your story.

## Pros and Cons of Editorial Calendars

Sometimes topics for pitches will be driven by editorial calendars, which are easy to find on publication websites. These schedules tell you what stories the magazine plans for the year and when they will run. An editorial calendar is a good resource, not only for upcoming topics and planned features, but to give you a sense of what the publication is all about. You can learn what the editors see as trends within the industry and what developments they consider worth a feature.

Editorial calendars aren't without their down side. Some pubs don't like to publish a calendar because it tips off the competition, and no one in the media likes to be scooped or copied. And if you see a planned feature that looks perfect for your company, rest assured your competition has seen it, too.

### Ideas From Your Own Head

Sometimes you are better off pitching an idea of your own that's not part of the published editorial schedule. Don't let that stop you if it's not on their list. These schedules aren't set in stone. No editor is going to turn away a good, solid story idea.

Case studies are always welcome as articles, especially if there is an interesting twist or remarkable result. But please, don't make it a promotional piece. Think like a journalist. If you have a number of case studies with a common thread, pitch it as a trend piece and pull from each case study as supporting examples. Has your company done some good white papers? They're also good for repurposing as articles.

### Google Me This, Batman

If you have an idea for an article, do a Google search of key phrases that relate to it and see what other articles or coverage comes up. Who knows what you'll find. Maybe the idea is more saturated than you realized. Maybe there's another angle you hadn't thought of. And maybe – probably – there are several publications you hadn't even thought of either.

For example, a marketer friend has a client who builds beautiful furniture from recycled barn wood. To pitch a story, she could search terms like recycled wood, recycled wood furniture, sustainable living, etc. You get the picture.

### Build a List of Topics to Pitch

Don't stop with just one idea. Keep building your list of topics so you will eventually have enough to fuel a steady stream of pitches. You may find something on one site that makes you think of an article you could pitch to another type of publication. Just don't pitch the same story to multiple editors at the same time. Best to approach them one at a time, unless they cover totally different markets.

# CHAPTER 9

## Marketing Toolkit – Industry Events

*Don't build links. Build relationships.*

— **Rand Fishkin,** Founder, *SEOmoz*

The exhibiting and conference business has taken a hit in the last decade or so, but there are still enough trade shows around to keep B2B marketers busy. This chapter focuses on some of the things you should consider in addition to ordering carpet and plants and hoping your demo staff shows up for their shifts.

## IT'S TRADE SHOW SEASON. HOW'S THAT PR PLAN?

### Get PR Back in the Picture

All too often, trade show PR gets pushed aside by all the other details of exhibit marketing. Smaller companies especially lack the bandwidth to focus on it, on top of all the other show arrangements. There's only so much marketing director to go around.

Show PR takes time, although it takes it in chunks, rather than big blocks of hours. Contacting press and analysts and setting up meetings (fondly known by some as "dialing for editors.") Negotiating mutually convenient times. Changing schedules at the last minute. Knowing the contact well enough to have an inkling of their interests and potential for flexibility. All this has to happen long before the first rental plant arrives and carpet installation goes down.

## Legwork and Heavy Lifters

It's true. You can set up an amazing press agenda without actually attending the trade show. That's because the upfront legwork happens before you even get there. Over the past decade, I've set up some pretty darn good PR schedules for clients at trade shows, and yet I have attended hardly a one! It's all about the legwork. You can't do any of this at the show anyway. If that's your plan, you've waited way too late.

I leave the grueling at-show pace to the heavy lifters on the show floor. These people truly work their tails off as they step up for the press meetings you set up weeks ago. Anyone who can stay mentally fresh hour after hour for several days (and nights) and still carry on an intelligent conversation has my admiration and respect. I've been there. I know what it feels like to will your brain to work.

That said, if you're the PR contact, you really should try to get to the show. You've got a pretty good excuse for the travel req.

## Not Budget Busters

One of the best things about show PR is, as a corporate marketer, you don't have add a lot to the budget to make some valuable contacts. If your company is already exhibiting, contacting and meeting the press is a small addition financially.

It ranges from next to nothing, if you do it all yourself, to about a day's work total for an agency. Even if you hold a press conference, rent a room, and provide refreshments, that expense can often be "dealed out" with event management or a nearby hotel. It's worth it for your company, and you can't match the media face time anywhere else. This is personalization at its best and frequently most enjoyable.

So the takeaway is: no matter what your resources and budget, don't waste this trade show opportunity to spend time with press and analyst influencers. Even short meetings with one or two key press can keep you on their radar and increase your credibility over the long term.

### Phases 1-2-3

Be aware of the three phases of conference PR: pre-show, at-show and post-show. While at-show activities can be very intense, most of the work takes place during the "before" phase. And the level of post-show PR depends on how well you did the first two.

## Trade Show PR — Only the Beginning

So there's this show. Your company is exhibiting. What do you do now? Start with these questions.

- Q Why is your company attending this show?
- Q Who attends that you want to talk to? Why should they care about what you are showing?
- Q Are you announcing anything new? Do you have significant announcements to make (It's ok if not. We can work around that. It's really all about relationships anyway.)
- Q Will you do a pre-show webinar? Why?
- Q Can you get the preregistered press list? (As an exhibitor, you have a right to this.)
- Q Is there a show daily and what are the deadlines?
- Q Are any press (i.e. publishing companies) exhibiting in booths? You'll want to visit them.
- Q What are your key messages for this show? What is your marketing theme? Again, ok if you don't have one.
- Q Pre-show: reach out to your own media circle and to the pre-reg list with an appealing email. The goal is to set up some meetings.

- Q Who is available to meet with press appointments and be onsite PR contact?
- Q Press kit: what's the plan? There are many things that might be included. Who will produce it? How many will you need? What's the format? Thumb drive? Online?
- Q Post-show: if you don't have any post-show PR assignments and follow-up, you haven't done enough PR at the show.

## It's Show Time! Make Yours Count

In spite of our pernicious "online-ness" and screen-centric work lives, trade shows still draw crowds. We like spending time with people who share our interests. We like the pursuit of profit in the public domain. It's an adult playing field for the game of commerce.

The size of the crowds seems to be open to continuous debate these days. Nevertheless, shows are unmatched for in-person face time with prospects, partners, clients and the press.

### Work the Plan

If you don't have a PR plan for every show, you're missing a chance to spend time with influencers who want to know more about your business – and who may know more about it than you do. Even if you just talk to a few journalists, you've spent time with people who matter to your company.

### Rule Number One

Rule number one is to remember that there's no busier time for a journalist or analyst than being on the road covering a major trade show or conference. Everyone wants a piece of them, so expect no more than 30 minutes of their time, if that. It's nothing personal.

## Reaching Out

Assuming you know your company's main messages and announcements for the show, start your pre-show outreach with your own industry press list. Also, since you are an exhibitor, ask for the pre-registered press list. This won't be much use to you until about three or four weeks out from the show, and then check in with your show contact every so often to get an updated list. (If you start too early with the show's "pre-registered" list, you might just end up with the list of journalists from last year.) Cross reference with your own list and see if there's any one else you should know.

Once you've got a real list of press attendees, send an email asking about their interest and availability for a short briefing at the show. Give them some tempting tidbits about your company's show plans to get them interested in meeting with you, but don't be too vague or cute.

## Setting Up Press Appointments

When you get a positive response, begin locking in appointments and filling in your master schedule. If there starts to be too much emailing back and forth on good times and bad times, just pick up the phone and call the writer.

Keep lots of notes about what the journalists want to talk about and who they will be bringing with them. If it starts to look like they want to have more of a sales meeting than a PR briefing, you need to step in and set expectations. Your executives aren't going to want to waste their precious time with an advertising sales pitch. You have to manage that.

## The Master Press Briefing Schedule

You know you are going to need some kind of schedule document, right? I'm a Word Table girl myself, but I suspect the majority of you are Excel trackers. It can be pretty simple, so use whatever works for you. The whole point is to put together a schedule of meetings that you or someone else will execute.

Even if you are planning to be the point person at the show, prepare your schedule as if someone else had to do it. You never know, it just might happen.

To make sure anyone can follow and execute the show PR schedule, be sure to include this information:

- Dates and show hours (get these from the show website.)
- Location of meetings – In your booth, the press room, lobby, whatever.
- Who will be the company point person for the meeting.
- What other experts or execs (not mutually exclusive) need to be available for a particular meeting.
- Hours – I split the schedule into mornings and afternoons and leave lunch open for the booth PR staff. They need the downtime, and they also like time to check out the show themselves.
- Topics for discussion – As you set up your meetings, ask if there are special topics the analysts or press want to cover. Include these as notes with the final schedule. This will also help you line up the best people from your company to talk to the press.

### A Friendly Reminder

Send an email to each of your press appointments a few days before the show. Include a reminder of the time and date of their appointment, the booth number or other location, who they should ask for, and a cell phone number of the show PR contact person. Sometimes I'll ask for the writer's number, too, and provide that to the company PR person in the notes section of the master briefing schedule.

### You'll Need Help

Keep everyone in the loop on appointments and expectations in real time. Executive admins and assistants will be your best friends when it comes to trade show bookings, because you want to know things like when the vice president of marketing gets into town. These special folks are the ones who know what limited hours the company president has for exclusive show briefings. Meetings with these senior execs are your "golden coin" appointments, so spend them wisely.

Provide the final, most up-to-date appointment list to your at-show PR contacts and anyone scheduled to participate in the briefings. Don't be surprised if some analyst or editor calls you the day before the show to set up an appointment. It happens.

### Any Surprises?

It's a good idea to poll everyone in your company you can think of about their show plans: new departments, overeager product managers, rogue marketers. There's always the odd announcement scheme that you don't find out about until the last minute.

Now you're ready for the at-show phase of your show PR. Be sure you have some press kits on hand in the booth for your briefings, as well as some for the press room.

## What Can a Conference Website Teach You About a Market?

Not only do conferences and events put you face to face with B2B buyers, these programs can also be a ready reference for learning more about certain markets and industries.

### Want Ideas About a New Market? Read a Conference Website.

Want a quick exploration of a particular vertical market? Maybe you're new to a job and want some ideas to kickstart a strategy.

Or it could be you're working your way through a job interview and want to sound knowledgeable about the hiring company's playing field.

There's a great, free resource waiting online that gives you instant insights into almost any market. Just "read" a conference. That is, identify a major trade show in the target industry and read the show website "cover to cover." You can learn a surprising amount about the market, its interests and its influencers — press, bloggers, analysts and customers — without even attending the show.

Study the trade shows if you need ideas for:

- Blog content
- Guest bloggers
- White paper topics
- Newsletter articles
- Webinar topics
- Insight into competitors' positioning
- Snapshot of industry trends

### Conference Deep Dive Turns Up Pearls

When I first start working with a new client, one thing I ask is what conferences do they and their customers attend? It's the starting point for a rich research deep dive, and it doesn't cost a thing.

The materials that industry conferences publish online are a fingertip goldmine of information and ideas. As an example, I looked up a SharePoint tech conference, SPTechCon. (SharePoint is a Microsoft collaboration, knowledge and productivity platform for enterprises.) This one turned out to be a motherlode of marketing ideas, far more than I expected when I chose it as my example. I didn't know much about the SharePoint market, but I came away with many good ideas for marketing to decision makers and influencers. And if SharePoint isn't your thing, you can still use these ideas, too.

## Let the Conference Do Your Research

Good show producers do their research and know what will interest the target audience. Take advantage of their hard work. Session tracks and presentation topics yield clear clues about the top concerns and interests of your target audiences. Study the agenda and tracks to get a sense of user problems and issues.

This SPTechCon show had dozens of sessions, so I tried to spot common themes. That led to the conclusion that hot topics for this audience include development, "Next Gen" SharePoint and how-to advice.

Also pay attention to what isn't being covered. If your product focus is on proofing or document composition, but there's nothing like that in the SharePoint conference agenda, that could mean an opportunity for you to claim that niche.

The courses yield ideas for developing content of your own, such as articles, white papers and webinars. Use the session descriptions as the starting points for outlines. The session speakers and their bios offer people to interview for newsletters or to approach for guest blogs.

## But Wait, There's More

Conferences and B2B trade shows are usually affiliated with a professional association. This gives us a few more reasons to keep these old standbys in our toolkit.

## Why Professionals Associations Make Good Marketing Sense

For the small price of the annual dues, you can join a group of professionals who share your interests. Yup, industry associations.

I love the dedication and enthusiasm you find in these groups. Few people join who don't care about the "cause." Also, associations are rich marketing tools, and that's what I want to talk about.

- Want **visibility**? Serve on committees or as an officer. Contribute to newsletters.
- Want **credibility**? Associations offer certification and training. Submit entries for an award.
- Want **recognition**? Association committees welcome and publicize people who are willing to contribute.
- Want **contacts**? Participate with kindred spirits interested in the world you sell to.

### 12 Ways **Associations Help You and Your Company**

If you're new to a market or just starting a career, joining an association will give you an instant circle of contacts and focused education on topics you should know about.

Here are some of the ways joining an industry association can help you as a marketer and a professional:

1. Exchange real life experiences and knowledge with your peers.
2. Build a base of people you can call on as sounding boards or focus groups.
3. Contribute to the community of knowledge. Earn thought leadership points.

4. Participate in seminars, workshops and conferences. Sometimes you can't find this training anywhere else.
5. Interact with industry leaders one on one. Sometimes you can't make connections like this anywhere else either.
6. Keep current with emerging technologies and best practices.
7. Develop your business skills like networking and running productive meetings.
8. Seek out opportunities to practice your leadership skills.
9. Mentor young professional and student members.
10. Receive discounts on products and services.
11. Show your commitment to the profession and influence its future.
12. Connect with other vendors in your space. Think referrals and co-selling.

### Network with Kindred Spirits

Think of the professional association as a club for influencers, evangelists, participants and networkers. No matter what you are interested in, there's probably a professional association committed to it. And if you're committed to the field, that's where you need to be, too.

Having said that, I've been in marketing a long time, dating back to the days when copy was written on an electric typewriter, and you could smoke in your office while you composed. (Hey, that was only for my first few years. I quit a long time ago.) In spite of my possible qualification as a dinosaur, let me say that social media and digital communication are the best thing to EVER happen to marketing. I am a total enthusiast.

Having said that, there are still two things that shouldn't and don't need to change. One is the need for good content. The second is, we're still people selling to people, and it's a good thing to actually see each other once in a while. Remember that early chapter on customers? Networking improves when you can connect in person. Conferences, trade shows, professional associations --- keep them all close to your heart, and your customers will be there, too.

# CHAPTER 10

## Marketing Toolkit – Marketology

*Marketing isn't magic. There is a science to it.*

— **Dan Zarrella,** Social Media Scientist, *HubSpot*

Let me start off with a disclaimer. I worship social media, but I'm by no means an expert. I embrace marketing automation, but I'm no geek. Technology and social media have transformed marketing, and forget "Mad Men." This is the Golden Age of Marketing.

If you're not using social or automating some of your processes, you've got some catching up to do, but don't be intimidated. Start slow, and don't worry that you didn't get into social media and the like sooner. Everything you would have done five years ago is different now anyway. It's never too late. I'm just a rookie, too, and here are some of my observations.

### Marketing + Technology = "Marketology"

What do these things have in common?

- Multi-channel communications
- Direct mail using personalized URLS
- Print advertisements using QR codes
- Email blasts
- Company websites
- Business blogs
- eNewsletters
- Video testimonials
- Optimized press releases

They are all very contemporary, very effective marketing tactics that depend on technology for their execution. I call it "marketology." There's very little we do today in marketing that doesn't benefit from a little behind-the-scenes coding.

### Marketing (heart) Technology

Marketing is stronger from the presence of its ally, Technology. Technology lets us track the effectiveness of our creativity. It lets us reach customers on their phones and on their desktops. And Technology would be dead in the water without strong, persuasive content. It's a marriage made in heaven.

## ALERT! ALERT! 12 WAYS TO USE GOOGLE ALERTS FOR MARKETING AND PR

Ever play around with Google Alerts? As a marketer, you should. They can work for you in many ways, and like so many great online marketing tools, they don't cost a thing. First, go to http://www.google.com/alerts to set up your account. You can set up one or multiple alerts, and specify things like send alert "as it happens" or batch them up daily or weekly. You can even choose the type of content you want Google to look for, whether blogs, news articles, videos or something else. You can ask for only the best results, or all results that match your keywords. So once you figure all that out, you'll be ready to fire up some Google Alerts to support your marketing strategies.

### 12 Ideas to Get You Started

Here are a dozen ways you can make Google Alerts add value to your marketing efforts:

1. **Track your keywords** – You do know what yours are, right? Find out how they are being used and by whom.
2. **Track your company** – Ditto.
3. **Track your competition** – Ditto

4. **Track a press release** – Not hard to do. Plug in selected key words from the release and hopefully you'll get results for your PR metrics.
5. **Build your press list** – Who's writing about topics and companies that align with your keywords? Should you add these people to your press list?
6. **Find ideas for article topics** – What's getting picked up by Google on specific keywords? This will give you ideas for articles to write with your company's own unique spin.
7. **Automate PR tracking** – This makes it so easy to track all kinds of PR presence. And it's frigging free, did I mention that already?
8. **Find opportunities to engage and expand your network** – When you see an interesting alert, send an email like, "Saw you quoted in XSY article about such and such. We also believe that is an important topic for our industry because..." and invite them to visit your website, blog, whatever. Maybe add them to your press list, if they're an influencer.
9. **Look for lead opportunities** – Similar to above. For example, if you provide eBilling services, you might set up an alert using the word "eBill." Reach out to companies that pop up in your alerts. Have a standard but customizable letter or email template that explains why you're contacting them.
10. **Discover trend leaders** – Who is blogging and covering your niche? Who's getting the coverage?
11. **Find award programs for your niche** – For example, plug in the keywords "software award." Who's winning? What did they do to win? Who gives out the awards? You'll learn a lot.
12. **Find content to share with others** – Who doesn't like receiving a great article about a subject that interests them? Share with your executives, your customers, your prospects, your colleagues.

### Great Time to Be a Marketer

If you set up alerts using powerful, relevant keywords, you'll get results that will benefit you in many ways. Now that I've alerted you to the possibilities, go on, set one up now. It will only take a few minutes, and you'll gain tons of value for your marketing efforts. And did I mention, it's free?! What a great time to be a marketer!

## Don't Give Up on B2B Blogging

Marketology has enabled one of my favorite B2B content marketing tools: blogging. Recently, a savvy software exec told me he'd been the company blogger for three years, but eventually dropped the task because no one was reading the blog. I have no doubt this person worked hard on his blog posts, and I was sorry the effort had been a disappointment. His experience made me re-examine my own commitment to the medium. Have I been wrong about the value of blogs to businesses?

### Still a Blog Believer

After some pro and con self-debate, I am still a believer in blogs. Done well, blogging is a powerful, versatile B2B content marketing tool — for most companies. Maybe it truly wasn't a good fit for my software friend or maybe there were other reasons his company blog didn't take off. If you've also tried and given up on B2B blogging, I would put these post mortem questions to all you less-than-satisfied former bloggers:

- Q How did you promote your blog?
- Q Did you announce new posts on Twitter and appropriate LinkedIn groups?
- Q Did you email posts and links to your customers and prospect lists?
- Q How do you know no one was reading it? Did you track open rates?

- Q Was the information useful to your audience?
- Q Did you turn the blog content into brochure-speak?
- Q Did you publish regularly?
- Q Did you ever comment on other blogs in your industry and link back to your own?

## Don't Stop — Instead, Make Your Blog Do More

If you're undecided about the value of B2B blogging for your company, don't give up. Instead, make that bad boy blog work harder. Here are some ideas for maximizing your blogging efforts:

- **Repurpose your blog posts** — Think about accumulating posts into an eventual white paper or eBook you could promote to your target markets.
- **Press releases** – Link to your blog from your press releases, and use the blog post to offer a little insight or background on your news. Inbound links are always good for your blog and website.
- **Talk about company activities** – Someone speaking at a conference or participating in a panel? Before and after the event, use the blog to talk about why the presentation or panel is relevant. Provide a summary of key messages from the presentation and put them in context of your industry and market trends.
- **New product primer** – You can't always convey your passion about a new product through your press release or product collateral. When you launch new offerings, include blog posts as part of the launch strategy. Bloggers can be the product managers who talk about why the product can help the target audience.
- **Guest blogging** – As an alternative (or supplement) to an in-house blog, what about finding opportunities for guest

posts on other industry blogs? Maybe your customers have blogs, too, and would welcome a guest post now and then.

- **Partners and customers** – Invite strategic partners and even customers to write guest posts. It gives them some good exposure, and shows the diversity of the information your company can bring to readers.

### Don't Give Up!

Give it a year, give it three, but give B2B blogging a chance — or at least maybe one more.

## Stay Loyal to Your Sweet Spot

### I Get Googled

I'd like to share a lesson I've learned about staying loyal to your sweet spot. Here's the backstory. Being a dutiful social media marketer, I experimented with a Google AdWords account. Not really knowing what I was doing (and still not sure) I set up campaigns for "marketing writer," "freelance copywriter" and other keywords of that ilk.

Nothing happens. About ready to cancel the experiment, I find I've been Googled and turned up in a search from a service outsourcing company in Belgium. I'm thrilled. Skyping with the owner for about an hour, I learn about their copy needs, then spend another hour on a thorough proposal for their website. Nothing happens.

### I Get Googled Again

Then, low and behold, I get another nibble, this time an investment coach comes looking for web copy. Again, I am thrilled, but by now, something has started nagging at me. While excited and flattered that I've been found through Google search, do these prospects fit my "sweet spot" of the over-extended B2B marketing director? Absolutely not.

## I Get It

If I'm not careful, I will become the victim of "scope creep." I don't know about you, but I have to scramble to stay on top of the work I already have from good clients who do meet my target profile.

## It's Okay to Say No

None of us has time to answer any and every call for help. As marketers, we need discipline to stay focused on the markets, clients, tactics and requests that will bring the most return. We need discipline to say "no" to the internal requests for this brochure or that press release.

Don't go chasing every shiny thing in social media. Don't spread your finite marketing energy across every type of communication that could possibly be created. Thin paint covers poorly, and you'll only have to go back and do it again. Don't be a scope creep.

# CHAPTER 11

## Marketing Toolkit – Industry Awards

*"Leadership comes when your hope and your optimism are matched with a concrete vision of the future and a way to get there. People won't follow you if they don't believe you can get to where you say you're going."*

— **Seth Godin**, Best-Selling Author, *Tribes: We Need You to Lead Us*

Nothing earns marketers cred with customers and the C-suite like winning an award. Go for them all, from top analyst rankings to editor's pick for products to recognition for marketing campaigns. And don't just win those awards. Put them to work.

### 15 Ways to Get More Mileage Out of that Industry Award You Just Won

**Wow, so your company won an industry award! Congratulations! Now what?**

You probably don't win a business award every day, so make the most of it. Here are 15 ways to get more mileage out of the achievement. (And even if you DO win awards all the time, you can still use these ideas. You'll just be really busy.)

1. This first idea is pretty obvious. Get the **logo** from the sponsor and use it in email signatures, presentations, ads,

direct mail, anything visual. If you really want to go out of the box, and you are "that kind of company," have t-shirts or coffee mugs made up for your employees with the logo on it.

2. **Email blast** the good news to your customers and channel partners with a note from your company president or CEO. Talk about some of the people in the company who helped contribute to the achievement. Play up the group that gave out the awards. Talk about what it means to customers (i.e. they clearly made a good decision to work with you, didn't they?)
3. **Email to employees** – Take a little different tone with your employees than with customers, but again, have it come from the Top Dog. Make it fun. Make it a little zany, if you are "that kind of company." Maybe tie in with the t-shirt or coffee mug surprise. Thank them for their contribution.
4. **Trade show signage** – Take that logo along with you to every show. Besides banners and big show signage, make stickers for products and staff badges, and tent cards for the info desk. And speaking of trade shows, make sure the release is in the show press kit for the next six months.
5. Develop a **keyword list** from your award submission. The nomination materials are usually fairly extensive, so there should be some good, pre-approved content to use. Make the list available to marketing, public relations, sales, web master, copywriters, and anyone responsible for describing your company to other people. These words won you recognition in your industry. Why wouldn't you want to keep talking about them in your marketing materials? Search, baby, search.
6. Write your own **press release**. The award presenters will most likely do one, but also prepare your own. Sometimes you have to pass these through the award gatekeepers. Even worse, they might have a template that you "have" to use, but try to make your release speak for your company. If you can,

get quotes from an industry analyst or better yet, a customer. Don't use the same ol' tired copy like "We are so honored to receive this blah blah blah." Frankly, that's boring, and it's a waste of an important release moment. This could be your fifteen minutes of fame. TRY to come up with a different way to talk about winning the award, something that makes the release fresh and interesting. Maybe use a Q/A format with a company executive about the market circumstances that made the award possible. Talk about the corporate strategy and vision that's reinforced by the win. Tie the award process and recognition into industry trends. Leverage the moment into thought leadership for your company.

7. Do an **executive interview** for your website – This could be an extension of your press release. In fact, you could do a lead-in to the interview in your release and send readers to your website to read the rest of it. Or maybe you post the rest of it as a video.

8. Do a **webinar** focused on the best practices, products, services, techniques or other achievements that won you the award. This is tricky because you don't want it to be salesy (is that a word? It's certainly a condition.) Your entry materials must have contained some persuasive information. Did you showcase a case study? A strategy? How can this be turned into something useful for your customers?

9. Write an **article** based on your webinar content. Have your PR person pitch it to appropriate industry publications. More thought leadership for you. Mention the award win in a discreet way that positions you as an expert on the particular topic. And remember those keywords.

10. **LinkedIn** – By all means, post this news to all your relevant LinkedIn groups and to your own company LinkedIn page. Take advantage of the link to send them to your website for that executive interview in Idea #7.

11. **Twitter** — Same thing here. It takes just a couple of minutes to send a Tweet. Maybe encourage Tweeters in your company to

send Tweets about how winning the award makes them feel. Remember those keywords!

12. Write something for your **internal and external newsletters** – Take that copy you wrote for the news release or webinar and mash it together into an article (or series) for your newsletter. Only this time, use more quotes and maybe some pictures.
13. **Blog** about winning the award. Again, think series, think informative, think fresh, think keywords.
14. Create a **presentation** for your sales force – Remember that submission content? For most award programs, it can't be promotional, but has to be quantifiable, innovative and above the crowd. Go back to that information and see how you can turn it into an informative presentation. Sales people love to talk about this kind of stuff with customers. Make it easy for them. The point is not to make it about the fact that you won, but to talk about the best practices and creativity that you won for. This presentation would also be the basis of the webinar mentioned previously.
15. Use that slide deck you created and post it to **SlideShare**. In fact, consider posting all your educational/thought leader presentations to SlideShare.

Winning an industry award is a well-deserved honor for your company. Use these ideas to squeeze every bit of value you can from it. You've earned it.

# CHAPTER 12

## Marketing Toolkit – Webinars

> *As marketers, we should be changing the mantra from always be closing to always be helping.*
>
> — **Jonathan Lister,** VP North America Sales, Marketing Solutions, *LinkedIn*

You *can* do good webinars. Ninety percent of the work takes place before the event, so if you get that right, you only have a ten percent chance left of screwing up! Just kidding. You won't mess up. Follow the tips in this chapter for a worry-free webinar. And start your journey by attending a few yourself. That's one thing about webinars, there's an unlimited supply of them to sample. You'll start to recognize the various components that you will be creating in yours. Hopefully you find some good examples and best practices to follow.

### What Should Your Webinar Be About?

What you want to do is understand what attendees need – it's all about them. If you've done persona work, refer to it to understand your target market's challenges. Use your sales colleagues as sounding boards for webinar ideas and for possible customers to participate. Attend webinars sponsored by your competition and other vendors in a space you want to get involved in. See what topics or problems keep coming up, and use that as a map to plan a series of webinars.

The key to webinars, like any type of content, is to give your audience something useful. Focus on one topic. Remember, it takes time to explain a complex B2B product or service, and longer when you put it in the context of a customer problem. Focus. Don't make your webinar all things to all people.

## Always Be on the Lookout for Ideas

Research and case studies are great foundations for webinar content. Tie them to an issue where you want to build thought leadership or raise awareness about your expertise. Think of it as a tutorial. Connect it to a technology you're trying to showcase (but keep it neutral – not a sales pitch.) Talk to the problem, and paint a picture of what the ideal solution looks like and why. Then wrap up with five or so minutes of how your product or service meets all criteria. Build a credible foundation of need or best practices, then come in and establish your credibility on the subject.

Always be on the lookout for topics. Keep an idea file.

- Keynotes or sessions at conferences
- Problems solved by new technologies
- New research
- A cluster of customer stories on a certain issue
- Feedback from customer councils

## Webinars and Selling

Webinars can be effective lead generators; some say the best, so you better believe webinars are about selling. Conversion can even be higher than for white papers. Webinars explain complex ideas or new technology that your sales team may not be comfortable talking about with customers. Sales can still be included the process by inviting their customers using special emails that you prepare for them.

## Who's Running This Show?

One thing you'll need to know very soon is how will you produce the webinar. It depends a lot on your budget. If you outsource,

$20,000 per webinar is a typical starting point, and that might not include a speaker fee. If you do multiple webinars with a vendor, definitely get a volume discount. If you use an outside vendor to host your platform, make them work for their money. Often these vendors are parts of publishing companies that have added this as a service. Having a vendor to produce your webinar can be a blessing and a curse, but mostly a blessing.

You can host webinars yourself. Many commercial online meeting platforms can be used for webinars. Check to see what platform your company uses and if anyone else in the organization uses it for webinars. The more you do it yourself, the better and more comfortable you'll get. Give it a try.

### Planning and Scheduling

Start planning two months out. This schedule assumes you have already found your webinar vendor or decided to produce it yourself. Start your planning with some questions:

- What's the goal of your event?
- Who's the target audience?
- Is the audience public, or will you make it a private, invitation-only event for customers and prospects?

Other early tasks will include:

- Defining your topic
- Writing your abstract
- Identifying and securing speakers and moderator
- Kickoff call with webinar team

Scheduling the actual webinar date to fall six weeks out from the kickoff call works well, but sometimes it's okay to start promotions just a month out from your event. Even three or so weeks out isn't too bad, if your topic is strong, and your target list is well aligned with it. If the topic is important to them, most people will sign up even just a few days in advance. I know I have. It's probably more a matter of relevance than timing. Consider the time of year as well. Vacation season and holidays can reduce your turnout.

## The Abstract: The DNA of Your Content

Everything starts with the abstract. It's one of the most important pieces and needs to be carefully written. Explain the problem, the angles and the solution in one page. This core will guide all the pieces of the webinar, from the promotional email to the registration page to the presentation content. Also, use this to get webinar approval within your organization. You or a good writer who knows your topic should write the abstract. Include three to six or so "What you will learn" bullets and a "Who should attend" statement. The latter will be the job titles you are targeting. Sometimes a vendor will take the copy straight out of the abstract for the emails and landing pages, so you might as well do it right.

## It's Up to You

Get involved with the abstract, speaker selection and content development. Don't leave it entirely up to the vendor. You may be the one person on the team who understands the link between the outside expert's field and your company's message, solution or positioning, and it's your job to make the connection. You will need to define the agenda and abstract and guide the content. Your vendor probably does not have the background to do this.

## 30-minute Format Is Common

I've always wanted to produce a 20-minute webinar, but haven't tried it yet. I think that length might stand out from all the other webinars and appeal to a busy business audience. Most webinars are 30 to 45 minutes with about fifteen minutes for questions. If you go with a panel approach with more than one speaker, a longer webinar might be best.

Figure you've only got 30 minutes of real presentation time, and that should be enough. Focus on just. One. Thing. This isn't a seminar. It's a webinar. People are busy, and if you're lucky, they'll stick around for your whole show. Use the time to drench your audience in your main concept. Send them away with clear, informative takeaways. If you do plan a pure product pitch, schedule it for the last ten minutes after the Q/A. Let the audience know that anyone who wants to hang around for that can do so. That way you won't lose the bulk of your audience during the main program, and they can listen to just as much as interests them.

### The Dialogue Model

One formula I like involves a simple dialogue between a moderator and one or more subject matter experts. The time goes quickly, and it's filled (hopefully) with information that can be easily followed and absorbed. Structure the program as a conversation between moderator and speaker about your very specific topic. It's the opposite of an "I present, then you present" snooze fest. That doesn't mean you won't have to script the speakers or rehearse. You must do both, but that only adds to a more natural, uninterrupted flow.

Seek out experts who can carry on an interesting dialogue for thirty minutes. You want them to talk *about* information on the slides, not read the slides. Customers, analysts and other outside parties are great if you can get them, but analysts can be expensive, and customers are hard to pin down. You might want to do this using a subject matter expert from your own company. It all depends. If you can find the right internal person, that's going to save you a lot of time and money. You can have successful webinars with just your own team, provided it's not a blatant sales pitch, and you let your speakers know you're there to help. Try to avoid irritating voices. No matter how good the content, a weird or boring voice will be a distraction.

## Speakers and Moderators

If you can, find a moderator who gets your space and audience. If not, experienced moderators who don't know your business can carry a webinar even if they aren't native to your industry. Think of the qualities of good interviewers like Larry King or Terry Gross. Sometimes the webinar vendor will provide the moderator as part of your package. It may be an outside expert or someone on staff, like an editor or writer who's familiar with the topic. Vendors often do a good job finding a moderator who understands the category, market and audience. See what they can come up with first.

If the top subject matter experts (SME) are too expensive, go down a layer or two. Look to Twitter and LinkedIn for speaker ideas, and also industry associations. These "second tier" moderators and speakers may be more affordable because they get valuable exposure of their own in the deal.

*Tip: Ask how much of the speaker fee, if any, can be included in the vendor's agreement. It can be helpful for budget control to keep it as part of a bundled arrangement.*

Once you've identified the players, you'll need at least one live call with you, the vendor, the speaker, the moderator and any internal experts who are involved. Encourage your internal speaker, moderator and experts to connect freely with each other. You want them to build a rapport, especially if you plan to use a dialogue-based format.

## Consider a Webinar Series

If you feel you have more content than you can cover in one webinar, consider a series of webinars, each dedicated to a 30-minute look at one aspect of your subject. Look at your marketing and sales strategies. Do your value proposition, differentiators, product offerings or customer problems break up into logical chunks? Each chunk can become a webinar.

Promote it as a series, too, so anyone who's interested is more likely to sign up for the rest of the programs. You've already got their attention, so keep them aware and planning to come back. If you just have fifty people or less attend all the webinars in your series, you are in effect nurturing those prospects across your series. It's a powerful way to build your story, especially if it's a complex sale.

Let's say you have management buy in to run a series of webinars because they really liked your abstract. Try to do least one per month. That's a smart plan, because you can build up a storyline about your specific area of thought leadership. You end up with a cohesive webinar library that can live on your website for further promotions.

Private series webinars to existing clients can become value-adds that educate about how what you offer helps their business. Invitation-only webinars help when you launch technology or products that the field team is not comfortable selling yet. Your subject matter experts can do the explaining more effectively, then sales can go back and huddle with the client about next steps.

## You'll Need Questions

Two areas of your webinar require questions. The first involves polling questions. Sometimes it makes sense to break up the webinar with an audience poll. You can tie it back into what was just discussed, or use it to lead into the next section. Ask the audience if they currently use the technology you're featuring, or do they struggle with the problem the expert is explaining? Most webinar platforms support polling questions. Keep it to three or less. Ask the webinar vendor to provide the names of the people who respond and what they said. Your sales team might find the information helpful. If you word it right, polls can also be qualifying tools. Poll results can also be the topic of a post-webinar blog or some social media commentary.

Another area you will need to write questions for is the Question/Answer section. This is a back up plan in case you don't get good questions or any at all. Write about eight to ten based on the webinar content. Have the moderator and speaker decide in advance who will answer each question. You may not need them, but it's better than dead air or awkward fumbling.

### Webinar Visuals Are a Little Different

Most webinars are auditory experiences, with the only visuals being what's on screen. You can't think of webinar slides in the same way you use PowerPoints in a room face-to-face with a live audience. In a webinar, the screen is all the audience has to look at. It's not like being in the same room with your speaker. It's like watching a television screen. Seeing the same slide for several minutes gets dull. Keep it moving. Generally, don't leave any one up for more than a minute.

Experiment with light-hearted or fun visuals that you move through quickly. You can get away with slides that are more detailed if they support the conversation. For example, charts of findings may stay up a bit longer if you're doing a research-based webinar.

### Marketing the Webinar

An external webinar expert can be a big help in promoting the webinar. In fact, this is one of the main reasons for seeking an outside resource. Your vendor will be responsible for promoting the webinar via email and on their website.

However, some (most) vendors have just superficial knowledge of your topic and market, so stay on top of all the content in the emails and landing pages. Remember to keep that abstract front and center. Don't hesitate to speak up if you think the messaging is off or if it's poorly written. Write it yourself if you have to, assuming you're a good copywriter. If not, get help from the copywriters on your team. It's important to get it right, even if you have to do it yourself. Don't be bashful. Your vendor knows a lot of things, but they don't know your business.

**Get Them to the Registration Page**

You may need two. Your vendor will do the main registration landing page, but you might need another one after the webinar if you're marketing the on-demand version yourself. Because your webinar is generally done under the auspices of your partner (publisher, digital media publisher, research organization,) the landing page will probably carry their brand, and that's okay because it creates a more objective, neutral setting, but as a "sponsor," you'll also provide your logo and your speakers' photos. Again, you may have to push them on the copy.

Private webinars will carry your brand, and you'll have to find someone to build the registration page. Most popular online meeting platforms make this easy. You have more control, but you also do more of the work.

For registration forms, work with your database or telesales team to determine what fields should go into the form, like first/last name, email, title and job phone number. This should align with the current contact structure in your database. The fewer the questions, the better. Too many, and people will bail before they even get started. Keep it to the basics. I've abandoned many a webinar registration form because of the endless questions.

Get the vendor to provide extra URLs for your own webinar marketing and tracking. Usually four is plenty: One for telesales, field sales, social media, and a blog. Make sure the vendor knows that any of those leads that come from your URLs don't count towards their goal.

Your vendor may suggest using content assets like reports as a registration bonus, especially if registration is lagging. If they offer a report or white paper as lead bait, make sure it's fairly current and relevant and not something they pulled off their website after a superficial search. Check that the assets aren't off message. It happens. Remember, they don't know your market like you do. If your company has some good reports or white papers that are relevant, by all means, use those as registration bonuses.

*Tip: As the actual webinar date approaches, it's reasonable to ask for the numbers from time to time to know how registration is populating.*

### Emails Are Your Invitations

Keep them simple. Keep them focused. Avoid fluffy marketing-speak. Use language that means something to your target audience. Explain the problem or opportunity, and then convincingly describe why this webinar will reveal some answers. Include the "What you will learn" bullets and the "Who should attend" statement from your abstract. The latter will be the job titles you are targeting. The email is usually something the vendor will prepare, mainly from your abstract.

### Watch Out for List Fatigue

Assuming your vendor has a good list to start with, you won't have to worry about list fatigue if you're just doing one webinar. It starts to become a problem as you do a series, and you keep promoting to the same pool. If the content is fresh each time, and the series builds out a story, then you might not have a problem. The difficulty comes when, for whatever reason, the list starts to go stale. You also don't know how often your vendor is mailing other webinar emails to the same list. Ask.

Webinar vendors are often part of publishing enterprises, and may have multiple databases for different audiences. A vendor with a variety of lists is a good thing. Ask how they nurture and care for their lists. Do they require business email addresses? How often do they scrub their lists? The best companies cleanse their lists regularly to verify the contacts are still at their same companies and roles. This is an expense for the webinar vendor, so not all practice good list hygiene.

### Ask for Social Media Support

Ask your speaker and moderator if they would do social media promotion for the webinar, like blogs, Twitter and LinkedIn and posting information about it on their own website. Offer to write something for them. It never hurts to ask. (Let me say here, being respectful and pleasant with your speakers and moderator will go a long way to getting good cooperation.)

Put your own social promotion together as well, and ghostwrite Tweets and LinkedIn posts for your employees to use. One of those extra URLs you got goes with these. Get on your company's blog schedule. Write at least one pre-webinar blog with webinar registration as the call to action. Focus the blog on the issue the webinar covers. Do a post-webinar blog about what the audience learned (or maybe what those polls revealed) and use the on-demand webinar as the call to action.

Do some internal promoting, too. Post something in the sales newsletter. Ghostwrite an email template for account managers to use to invite customers (use that special URL you got from the vendor.) Keep your boss well informed about ongoing registration numbers (and final results), so she can talk up the webinar with her peers and boss.

### Should You Blow Your Own Horn?

Should you blow your own horn in your webinar? This sounds like an odd question. Doesn't talking about you go against all the cautions of "make it about the customer, not about your company"? On the other hand, you're paying for this event. Shouldn't you get something out of it?

Try for somewhere in the middle. If you're sponsoring a webinar, attendees expect you to have some skin in the game. They may have registered because of your company's involvement. They've done some research on the topic (maybe already attended some of the analyst-based webinars) and now they're looking for information to move along in the decision process. B2B buyers today look to brands and vendors for information, so give them your expertise, not your sales pitch.

If you can provide real information to help a customer understand and solve a problem, by all means, show off your company's knowledge and experience. Bring your customers and subject matter experts to the attendees. (Another reason to use internal talent is budget. Analysts and other celebrity speakers get very expensive.) People want to hear about the vendor side now. They look to your webinar to tell them how your company fits into the topic, how you can help solve their problem. It's not taboo anymore to talk about your company. It ties back to where attendees are in their buying process. If people have signed up for the webinar knowing your company has branded it, they obviously want to hear from you. One way to approach it is to tell the audience upfront that following the main portion of the webinar, they can stick around to talk specifically about how your company solves the problem. The people who stay are people you want to make connections with. They've self-qualified.

## The Downside of Celebrity Speakers

Attendees who would go to a webinar featuring an analyst or celebrity speaker are likely earlier in the sales funnel, than those who sign up to hear your perspective. If you sponsor a webinar with an analyst speaker, your conversion rate may be lower, because attendees are there to hear the expert, not your perspective. Celebrity speakers are draws for companies that need exposure, but may be a waste of money for established brands. When major analysts are the draw, the promotions give you people who are less engaged in what you have to say. Frankly, you probably want your company's expertise and topic to be the draw, because attendees will be better positioned in the buying cycle.

## Webinar Reporting: What's a Lead?

Note that by "leads," I am referring to qualified registrants. Technically, they may not be warm leads until someone does follow-up qualifying, but humor me here, and let's agree to call them leads.

- What constitutes a qualified registration? Be very specific up front, because you'll be sorry later if you have to eliminate a third to a half of your leads because they're from competitors or companies that you don't want to sell to. If you didn't make it clear to your vendor, bad on you.
- Always use filters. Tell your vendor in writing what the filters are, such as company size or certain titles. You can't stop people from attending, nor should you attempt to, but you can stop them from getting on your qualified lead list. The vendor should guarantee qualified leads to the filters, not to the unfiltered attendee list. Say you get 400 registrants, but not all meet the criteria. If you've got the right lead filters in place, only the good registrations will count.
- What's the back-up plan? What if the vendor doesn't deliver the leads they promised? Most agreements include extended time to hit your goal. Give them the opportunity to capture the remaining leads by marketing the on-demand version, within 30 to 60 days. The vendor will usually provide a batch of leads every week until they hit the target.

## That Doesn't Count

You may want to exclude registrations from the "gold list" that:

- Fall below a certain employee or revenue level. Consult with Sales to find out their cutoff levels. You don't want to generate a bunch of contacts that Sales won't touch. If the webinar will be marketed internationally, ask your colleagues in Europe, Canada and other markets, too. They probably have different criteria than U.S. sales.

- Come from competitors. You need to give the vendor a list of banned competitors. Sales, product marketing, research and others can help you put this list together. If you're doing multiple webinars, the competitor list could change depending on your topic. Always recheck your list when there's a new webinar.
- Use a personal email. If it's not a business email with company domain, it's probably a waste of time as a large, complex sale lead.
- Appear too junior – maybe. In large-scale B2B sales, everyone wants to reach senior-level executives and the C-suite. Most webinar attendees will have titles of manager and above. That's okay. These people are the gatekeepers who, if they find your information useful, will push it up the food chain to their bosses. Keep your title filter somewhat open in the beginning and close the lens down as you do more webinars, if you need to. You'll want to complete two or three to compare and evaluate the attendees. Better to be too open than too exclusive.
- Come from employees of your company or subsidiaries. This is obvious, but I point it out anyway. These numbers can add up, but never discourage your own fellow employees from attending. For one thing, if the webinar turns out well, you've just gotten a lot of exposure for your personal brand.

Get all this detail into your vendor's SOW, as in "scope of work."

**Reporting for Duty**

If you do your own webinar, you'll have to do all the reporting yourself. Let's assume though that you're working with a vendor. Here are some things to discuss about the leads and reporting.

Q When do you get the leads report? Anywhere from 24 to 48 hours is common. The vendor wants to scrub and rank leads for qualified vs. not.

- Q How will you get leads from the vendor? Usually a spreadsheet is okay, but check with whomever is getting the lead handoff to see what format they require.
- Q Does the lead report distinguish between live attendees vs. those who registered but didn't show?
- Q Does the lead report include who asked questions in the webinar? Can you tell if the questions were answered? This information can be useful. Telesales or field sales experts can use it to craft a follow-up call. You will be alerted to any issues you didn't realize people had with the topic, or new areas to explore in future webinars. You can use questions as a starting point for blogs, Tweets and LinkedIn posts. (Never let anything go to waste!)
- Q How many minutes did each person attend? Most platforms can tell you this live during the webinar, and it's a good measure of the appeal of your content. You'll learn if your content was on point. A low-attendance webinar that held its audience through to the very end might be better than a large audience that bailed out quickly.

Did I say this already? Get all this detail into your SOW.

## After the Webinar

Although you can start nurturing while still doing webinar promotion, it might get a little annoying and "stalky" to your registrants. Definitely do post-webinar nurturing. A typical campaign has two branches and several touches, depending on whether the person attended or not. For attendees, get them started on white papers, case studies or other assets relevant to the topic. Non-attendees would start out with a link to the on-demand webinar (you can do that with registered contacts, too, but you'll need a different email.) The main work at this stage is the brainpower to write good email copy that pulls people through a decision process. And that's moving out of the webinar realm, so we won't go into it in any more detail here.

If you have a telesales team doing follow-up, write the script for their calls. They will appreciate it, and you can establish continuity between the webinar and the next step. Have a version for attendees and one for no-shows. Tie it in with the webinar content, but lead them to the next point in your selling story. Think of an additional information asset you can send to move prospects along their buying journey. Again, the first asset for the no-shows is the link to the on-demand webinar.

### No Shows? No Problem.

Just because two-thirds of your registrations don't show, by no means get discouraged. Catch them through telesales follow-up or when your vendor sends the follow-up emails with the link to the recorded webinar. I only attend live about one out of every hundred webinars I register for, but that doesn't mean I'm not interested. It just means I'm busy or traveling. If you have the right content, people will listen at some point. It doesn't matter if it's live or later, because you've got their contact information.

### Repurpose Content with a Webinar Transcript

Push to get a transcript included in your SOW for delivery soon after the webinar. Street value of a transcript is only a couple hundred bucks, so don't let the vendor snow you with their estimate. If you have to, and their price is too high, get the recording and hire a transcription service to do it for you. It's worth the money. You can quickly turn it into other assets like blogs or white papers. Did I say this already? Never let anything go to waste.

### Consider International Audiences

Due to issues with time zones and translations, on demand webinars may work best if you want to do something in other countries. Many people consider on demand webinars best practice anywhere anyway. They are certainly easier to deal with, but you've still got to do the live webinar at some point. Live webinars simulcast in multiple countries get complicated fast, and in the end, people want to watch it when they want to watch it anyway. Don't stress out trying to make it work live everywhere.

Some points to remember for your vendor checklist for international webinars:

- What countries do you want to include, and what countries can the vendor support?
- What languages will you need? Any additional fees for translations? Will it be voice over or subtitles? Don't forget translations for registration page and email.
- What is the additional lead guarantee for each country?
- How will the webinar be promoted in-country? Where do they get their email lists? Regulations are different in Europe regarding emails. Be sure your vendor is on top of the latest rules.
- What's the promotion lead time for the different countries you want to reach?

### Webinar Vendor Checklist

As you evaluate vendors, ask about these things:

- ✓ Track record and case studies of successes
- ✓ Landing page for registration
- ✓ Email promotions and reminders
- ✓ Event platform
- ✓ Project manager for your account
- ✓ Producer or engineer for live webinar
- ✓ Qualified, engaging moderator
- ✓ Advice on speaker presentations
- ✓ Recommendations on on-screen visuals
- ✓ Commitment to specific number of qualified registrations
- ✓ What audience can they provide, given your filters
- ✓ Editorial asset tie in
- ✓ Social media promotion
- ✓ Promotion on their website
- ✓ International webinars, simulcast or other capabilities?
- ✓ Translations
- ✓ Transcript of webinar and Q/A
- ✓ Attendee reporting
- ✓ Post-webinar lead nurturing
- ✓ Webinar archiving and for how long
- ✓ Thank you emails to attendees and non-attendees

## What's Next for Your Webinar?

Webinars are worth the expense (which doesn't have to be a lot,) because they can be used in many ways. If you produce them yourself instead of hiring a vendor, the return on investment is even greater. Webinars can be repurposed as:

- On-demand assets in a special portal
- Reasons for a sales or nurture email
- Content syndication assets
- Podcast fodder
- Website material

Anywhere you'd use a white paper, you can almost always use a webinar, too. They meet the need for having a variety of content types in your marketing toolkit.

## Keep at It

The more webinars you do, the better you get. The first one will be intimidating, but follow your plan and focus on content. If you succeed in communicating your message, and you have the right audience, moving some of them along the buyer's journey is inevitable.

# CHAPTER 13

## Marketing Toolkit – Presentations

> "*Creating an interesting presentation requires a more thoughtful process than throwing together the blather that we've come to call a presentation today. Spending energy to understand the audience and carefully crafting a message that resonates with them means making a commitment of time and discipline to the process.*"
>
> — **Nancy Duarte,** President & CEO, *Duarte Design*

It's safe to say that somewhere in the world at any given time, someone's giving a PowerPoint presentation. This now-basic marketing activity gives companies an opportunity to spend quality time with customers, prospects and influencers. The sad reality is, most opportunities are wasted on clotted masses of visuals, bullet points and complete sentences. You can change that starting now.

### Stop Picking on PowerPoint

We hear "Death by PowerPoint," and everyone nods knowingly. Such extreme treatment! And it's wrong. PowerPoint doesn't kill audiences; presenters with bad PowerPoints do.

It's been my experience, that people WANT to see slides, but they want to see GOOD slides. That's the root of it. Quit messing around with goofy PowerPoint theories and excesses, and learn to create a decent slide deck. Or hire someone to do it for you.

### Work the Power

PowerPoints still have power. In fact, with things like SlideShare, they are more useful than ever.

There are several schools of presentation thought these days:

- One is to ditch the PowerPoints altogether. From now on, we *talk* to customers, no slide decks. Well, maybe we should have been talking to customers all along and not reading slides.
- There is a persistent style of turning each slide into a visual essay. Enough with the bullets already. Twenty may be just a few too many for one slide. Best practice is more like three.
- Then there are the minimalists who just want to use pictures and hardly any words. Some of the best presenters are known for using this technique.

Being the "slide person" is not a bad way to build up job security and run elbows with the executives. Presentation builder for the CEO has a nice ring to it, no? Get handy with PowerPoint. It's a good, basic skill to have, and you can be smart and creative to boot.

### Make a Stand for Presentation Best Practices

Marketing writers often get tagged to create slides for someone else. How often does a presentation project wind up on your desk? If you're lucky, you'll get to control it from the beginning. More likely, you'll be asked to "just spruce up" the Frankenstein slides someone else has started. For the purpose of this chapter, let's assume things are going your way today, and you've got a clean slate to build a presentation.

Be glad you can get your hands on it. Most corporate presentations go against every best practice known to man. You'll do your speaker and your company a favor if you can get it under control. You may be overruled, but try anyway.

Companies use presentations in many ways. The next one you work on may be:

- Hosted on an intranet portal for sales and service teams to download
- Part of a launch package for new offering
- For an executive who needs a conference presentation
- Posted on social media sites like SlideShare
- Used as a continuous loop on a kiosk or demo station

Whatever the purpose, treat it as any other marketing communication. That means you've got to answer some basic questions. Before you start, ask:

Q Who is the audience?
Q What customer problem does this slide deck relate to?
Q How much do they already know about the topic?
Q What do I want the audience to think or do after they hear this?

## The Contrarian Approach to Presentation Building

This may not come as a surprise, but I don't do presentations like most marketers. Most people start with the slides, and they get bogged down in the graphics right away. They get sidetracked by cool builds and stock images of giddy executives, and before you know it, you've got a monster on your hands. Instead of having the discipline to use PowerPoint as it was intended, as a talking guide, the space on the slide becomes a crutch. Everything the speaker wants to say gets added to the slide. We've all endured too many presentations built that way. It's a mess, and it doesn't serve the audience at all.

## Put Content First

Here's a different approach that starts with the content, then the script and then lastly, the slides. Because you're building it "backwards," the content distills down until only the high-level message appears on the slide. The details live in your script in the notes section. I can't tell you how many times I've scrolled through someone's presentation draft and been shocked to find "click here to add notes" in slide after slide. It's not fair to the person who must present your slide to not get a talk track.

What you say is the most important part of your quality time with customers. It's not the charts and bullet points, or the photos of happy employees smiling at their laptops. It's not professional to cram the script into the slide. Anytime you see a complete sentence on a slide, stop and drop it into the notes section. Replace it with a couple of words at most. The speaker will know what to say, because it's in the talk track. The audience doesn't need to read it, too. In fact, if the presentation is written out in the slides, who needs a presenter? Just let the audience read it. But then you don't get any quality time. And every relationship needs that.

The techniques described here focus on the content, the words, not on the graphics. I don't claim to be a designer. That I leave to the professionals and other books. Once you get to the graphics stage in your presentation, ask your marketing design team for help. Your company may have a brand department that also has approved visuals. As for what you want to say in the presentation, let me share the approach I take.

## 18 Steps to a Content-driven Presentation

1. Start with gathering all the raw content you can find on the topic. This might come from interviews, white papers, case studies, even watching an expert do a presentation on the same topic. Tape it or take lots of notes and use that content to create yours.

2. Slowly go through and organize the content into sections by topic. At this point, don't worry about the order of presentation. Long sections or short, it doesn't matter yet.

3. If you have an outline, plug in the raw content where it makes the most sense. I don't use outlines much myself. Instead, I let the organization flow out of the raw content. Don't worry about wordsmithing yet either. This step is about sorting your mess of content. Move quickly and don't overthink. You can't break anything.

4. As you roughly organize sections by subject, go through and give every section a rough headline. It doesn't have to be clever. It's part of the sorting process.

5. Now go back and organize the sections by beginning, middle and end.

6. You want sections to be one or two paragraphs. If any are longer than that, see if you can break them down into further sections with headlines. You may be starting to get the idea that each section is going to be a slide, but forget I told you that for now.

7. At this point, you should have a document full of short sections with rough headlines organized in the approximate flow of your presentation.

8. Go back through it again and rewrite each section in a light, conversational tone. Imagine you are saying it to someone, instead of reading it. That's exactly what's going to happen, because this is becoming your talk track. This step will take a while, but the copy still doesn't have to be perfect. You'll have plenty of time for that.

9. Next go back through and jazz up the headlines, but keep them short and simple. These are going to be the headlines of your slides. Now might be the time to get a reality check on your content. Nothing worse than writing the last bullet point on the final slide and finding out that wasn't what the boss was looking for. Here's how I like to share the content at this

point. Create a two-column table in Word. Drop your section headlines in the first column, and the talk track copy in the second column. Share this document for your first review. After you have sign off on the direction and topics, you're ready to open a new PowerPoint file.

10. Finally, we're getting to the actual slides! Your company or department may have a template you will use, or the project may have its own style. Find out what format you must use before you get too far into it. It's a bitch to have to change midstream.
11. Put in a placeholder for the title slide or build it if you already know it. Same for the closing, Q & A or "Thank You" slide.
12. Take each section of copy you created, and drop it into the Notes section of one slide. One section per slide. Pop the section's headline up into the slide's title placeholder.
13. From your notes, pull the key phrases that will help your speaker explain that slide's point. You don't need to include the entire talk track in the actual slide. If people wanted a brochure, they could read one. Don't cram everything into one slide. Just use enough copy to help the speaker remember what needs to be there to communicate the basic point of that section copy to the audience. If your notes are conversational, with just a little rehearsal, your speaker will be able to pull it all together just from looking at the slide points.
14. Repeat this step for all your slides. Then, put it all away and don't look at any of it for 24 hours. Don't even think about it. The difference a fresh look can make is amazing.
15. If your presentation runs long, say over ten slides, I like to create divider slides, just to break it up. If your slide deck is running longer than 20 to 25 slides for a 30 minute speaking slot, do some serious thinking about what you've included. Can you consolidate some slides? Is there any redundancy? Anything that doesn't really fit after all?

16. Once you have your slides laid out with copy points, then you can start thinking about your graphics. Follow the style defined by your company brand guidelines if you have them. Otherwise, keep them simple. They shouldn't overwhelm the content, but they can be bold. If you've got graphic artists on your marketing team, now's the time to bring them in. Correction. A few days *before* this would be the time to bring them in. Give them the head's up what's coming and ask them if they have time to help. Giving someone a little lead time can make all the difference.
17. Who's got to approve the deck? The speaker? Your brand department? Your boss? Review. Revise. Repeat. Hopefully, since you got the content and flow signed off earlier, any feedback won't knock you completely off the rails.
18. Will your presentation be posted on a portal for sales to download? Here's a tip. Have an internal expert do a recording of the final presentation. It might be the Sales Vice President or a Product Marketing Manager. Post this on the sales portal, so account executives can model their delivery after the expert's presentation.

### "Can I Get a Copy of Your Slides?"

Have you ever sat through a half-decent presentation where someone *didn't* say, "Can I get a copy of your presentation?" Hello, can you say marketing opportunity?

Instead of sending them the speaker's version, create two versions of your deck. One is the minimalist slide deck to present. The other is the handout or leave behind that contains everything you wanted to dump into the deck, but didn't. (This is less likely to occur if you know there will be a handout version.) Include contact information in this version. You never know who might share it, and you do want follow-ups, don't you? Add some hyperlinks to related content on your website. And be glad your speaker has one more invitation to engage with this prospect.

## Don't Give Up on Presentations

Don't give up on poor PowerPoint. Just because people do slides so badly doesn't mean they can't be done right. Give the ideas in this chapter a try. You may be surprised when you start getting feedback about that great that presentation you did.

# SOME FINAL WORDS

> *Be passionate about the culture and the business, and remain positive, because it inspires others.*
>
> — **Barry Libert**, CEO, *Mzinga*

## The Marketing Tribe

You're never an island in marketing. There are always unavoidable connections between you and other areas of the business: Sales, Finance, the C-suite, sometimes even the Board of Directors wants to get their hands in marketing. Those budget battles and diplomatic compromises are the responsibility of marketing leadership.

The marketers in the trenches, where the work gets done, that's where the real craftsmanship takes place, but it's never easy. Whether it's trying to make a snoozer of a product into something a buyer will care about, to racing around doing last minute arrangements for press meetings, to crossing your fingers and going live with a high-profile webinar, It's often stressful, and sometimes the only thing that helps relieve the tension is a perfectly timed wisecrack.

Marketing teams don't have superstars. One person alone can't get it done. A company with a single marketer is either just starting out or soon to be saying good-bye to one very burned out employee. I've seen people try to do it all, but it's not fair to you, the company or your customers. Your message and story – and your customers – deserve better treatment. It takes a tribe of smartass marketers who observe, comment and perform with equal measures of intelligence and wit.

On the other hand, one rarely sees a company with too many marketers. If anything, teams tend towards the lean side with everyone running and gunning, learning as they're burning. These harried groups will find this book useful. If you base your marketing toolkit on the ideas in this book, you'll have most of your bases covered. If you don't have to spend so much time worrying about "what do we do?" you'll have more time to think about "what do they want?" and "what do we say?"

Even so, the idea of having to do all these things: press releases, white papers, case studies, webinars, trade shows and so on, might overwhelm you. Well, you've got to do them anyway. The thing is, all these tactics connect you with the customer. Pick a few things to focus on to start and pour all your energy into doing them right. Once those are running on autopilot, pick up another tool, get a sense of it and plunge in. Go with your strengths. If you've got strong writing resources, go heavy on content marketing. If your product is something best seen in person, like heavy equipment or large printing systems, exhibit marketing gives the necessary hands-on your decision makers require. If you've got a service to sell an emerging segment like enterprise mobility, white papers and press releases can frame the issue in your terms and educate buyers about all the nuances of the issue.

By doing SOMETHING, you meet the needs of B2B customers who want to learn how your business can solve problems for them. You're not just marketing to customers. You're marketing *for* them. They want to know about solutions to their problems. If your company truly fits their situation, you will get their attention. Make a connection. Raise interest. Gain consideration. Create preference. Then hand it over to Sales.

You might wonder if I have any favorite tools from this handbook. I've had success with all of these, and in the process, learned a lot. Above all, I'm into content. It doesn't really matter so much what the interface is between you and the customer, if you stand there (figuratively speaking) when you have the chance, and stumble over your story, what a wasted opportunity. Saying it right so customers get it, that's so hard, yet so important. I've seen countless campaigns where well-meaning marketers pour their souls into all the stages of their nurturing campaigns or the details of content syndication, and what's always the last thing on the agenda? The content – the words you use to speak to the customer. It's like putting all your worry into the pen and paper and ignoring what you are going to say. Put the message first always. Correction. Put the customer's need first, and the message second.

I don't pretend that this is the bible of B2B marketing. It was never intended to be, but I do know you'll find things that will make your life easier. The advice, tips and ideas in this book will relieve some of the pressure of your day-to-day marketing grind. If you're trying to figure out what to do, browse through a few chapters. Something will come to you, I promise. It's not necessarily strategic, but in reality, who really follows that marketing plan anyway? Most real-world B2B marketing is reactive. The advice and ideas in this handbook will help not only you, but also your team get more done more effectively, leaving more time for snarky jokes and beer.

# ABOUT THE AUTHOR

## Who Is this Carro Ford?

When I was growing up in "Luh-vul," Kentucky, going to Catholic girl school, I never dreamed I'd turn out to be a marketing expert. I didn't even know what Marketing was until I was out of college, and somehow landed in the Mobile, Alabama marketing department of a regional bank. Looking back, I don't see how I could have been anything but a marketer.

There's no career with so many angles, so many industries, so many different paths, and I've explored many of them. Proudly I claim my "geek" status. I've been in marketing my entire career. Most of that has been in B2B technology, aside from what turned out to be an eight-year stint in bank marketing – my first real job.

My serpentine career path has flowed between corporate and consulting worlds. Sandwiched between corporate jobs, I ran my own PR and content agency for 14 years, and I still keep a handful of freelance clients.

I've connected with many B2B marketers, from multi-national public companies to smart start-ups, from the international clients I've still never met face-to-face, to the ones who've become close friends. I've worked for marketers in pharmaceuticals, business training companies, manufacturing, professional associations, trade publications, virtual office firms, research organizations, business services, plastics extruders, logistics companies and call centers.

Always at the heart of it was writing, from the early jobs in radio news and bank marketing, to my first tech marketing job in the early eighties when it was all getting started. (I even saw Bill Gates once in Las Vegas at a Comdex afterhours event. All I remember is that his loafers were scuffed.) I tell you with confidence, I can write anything needed for business-to-business marketing: press release, case study, white paper, web content, brochure, presentation, letter, email, blogging, and more. When people ask how I learned to write, the answer is that I learned by reading. I'm a passionate reader and can hardly go a day without it.

Marketing isn't just a job; it's my professional passion, my hobby. Work has never felt like work—more like a puzzle to solve. I never get bored with writing, because there's always something I can do to make each piece just a little crisper, a little fresher, a little tighter. Every day is a new opportunity to sharpen my saw and learn how to combine good content with the latest tools and strategies. I'm not a frustrated fiction writer, because to me, marketing copy is the ultimate in creative writing.

And one more thing. What's up with "Carro"? What kind of name is that, you ask. Here's the story. I was named for my great-grandmothers, Carro Shannahan and Susie Ford, both hardworking farm women. I've heard nary a cross word about Susie, but family lore has it that Carro was a bitch who cheated at cards. I bet she was a smartass, too.

Want to talk more about B2B marketing? You can reach me at *carrof@earthlink.net* or on LinkedIn.

# ACKNOWLEDGEMENTS

A huge sigh of gratitude and relief to La Heather. Heather Joan Marinos was the wise engine that turned my mess of thoughts into a real book and guided me through the labyrinth of becoming a self-published author.

Thank you to Sheryl Pattek for graciously agreeing to write the foreword for this book. (You'll always be the "CMO Whisperer" to me.)

Thanks to Gina Burns, cover illustration artist and past colleague who always had too much class to be a smartass. Here's a plug for GG's worthy cause: treatmentbeforetragedy.org.

To BHW, thanks for reminding me that marketing is a profession that thinking people might actually find interesting and want to understand.

To Sean and Aiden, Aiden and Sean, who knew enough by grade school to push my buttons with, "Oh Mom, that's just marketing."

To Alma Oliver Corley, R.I.P., for giving me my first ever marketing job before I even had a clue what marketing was. You took a chance on that clueless college graduate, and I hope she's made you proud.

To all the smartass marketers I've worked with, I'm grateful for your support, encouragement, understanding, wit and gumption, and if I can ever do anything for you, please let me know.

# BIBLIOGRAPHY & SUGGESTED READING


Albee, Ardath. *eMarketing Strategies for the Complex Sale.* New York, New York: McGraw-Hill, 2009.

Breakenridge, Deirdre K. *PR 2.0: New Media, New Tools, New Audience.* Upper Saddle River, New Jersey: FT Press, 2008.

Carroll, Brian. *Lead Generation for the Complex Sale.* New York, New York: McGraw-Hill, 2006.

Gallo, Carmine. *The Presentation Secrets of Steve Jobs: How to Be Insanely Great in Front of Any Audience.* New York, New York: McGraw-Hill, 2010.

Gladwell, Malcolm. *Blink.* New York, New York: Little, Brown and Company, 2005.

______, *What the Dog Saw*, New York, New York: Little, Brown and Company, 2009.

Halligan, Brian and Dharmesh Shah. *Inbound Marketing.* Hoboken, New Jersey: John Wiley & Sons, 2010.

Handley, Ann and C.C. Chapman. *Content Rules.* Hoboken, New Jersey: John Wiley & Sons, 2012.

Heath, Chip and Dan Heath. *Made to Stick.* New York, New York: Random House, 2008.

King, Stephen. *On Writing.* New York, New York: Scribner, 2010.

Kantor, Jonathan. *Crafting White Paper 2.0*. 2009.

Levine, Rick, Christopher Locke, Doc Searls, and David Weinberger. *The Cluetrain Manifesto*. Philadelphia, Pennsylvania: Basic Books, 2009.

Lizotte, Ken. *The Expert's Edge*. New York, New York: McGraw-Hill, 2008.

Masleny, Andy. *Write to Sell*. London: Marshall Cavendish Limited, 2009.

Meerman Scott, David. *The New Rules of Marketing and PR*. Hoboken, New Jersey: John Wiley & Sons, 2008.

Ogilvy, David. *Ogilvy on Advertising*. New York, New York: Random House, 1985.

Plotnik, Arthur. *Spunk & Bite: A Writer's Guide to Bold, Contemporary Style*. New York, New York: Random House, 2007.

Pulizzi, Joe and Newt Barrett. *Get Content. Get Customers*. New York, New York: McGraw-Hill, 2009.

Ries, Al and John Trout. *Positioning: The Battle for Your Mind*. New York, New York: McGraw-Hill, 2001.

Schaefer, Mark. *The Tao of Twitter*. New York, New York: McGraw-Hill, 2012.

Stelzner, Michael. *Launch: How to Quickly Propel Your Business Beyond the Competition*. Hoboken, New Jersey: John Wiley & Sons, 2011.

______, *Writing White Papers*. Poway, California: WhitePaperSource Publishing, 2007.

Truss, Lynne. *Eats, Shoots & Leaves*. New York, New York: Penguin Books, 2003.

Weber, Larry. *Marketing to the Social Web*. Hoboken, New Jersey: John Wiley & Sons, 2009.

# APPENDIX A
# So You Want to Be a Freelance Writer?

*"Advertising is a business of words, but advertising agencies are infested with men and women who cannot write. They cannot write advertisements, and they cannot write plans. They are helpless as deaf mutes on the stage of the Metropolitan Opera."*

— **David Ogilvy**, "The Father of Advertising"

## So You Want to Be a Freelance Writer?

Good choice, but like anything, you gotta pay some dues. Don't worry. This time spent learning the trade in the business world can be kind of fun, and it's absolutely necessary.

For starters, let's assume you can write. Next, here's what I would do to build a career as a freelance writer. (In fact, this is exactly what I did do.)

### Want to Be a Freelancer? Then Get a Job.

I know you want to immediately experience the glamour of the freelance lifestyle, but when you're a rookie, it pays to start your career at a real company. Get an entry level marketing job in a corporation or agency. Think of it as a paid internship. This will pay off because:

- You'll learn how to work with and satisfy internal and external clients.
- If the organization uses freelancers, you can learn from them.
- You can get your employer to pay for various professional certifications.
- You can build experience in a niche or specialty market, which is the way to go as a freelancer.
- You'll make lifetime friendships. My best buds are people I met years ago at some of my first "real" jobs.
- You might decide freelancing isn't for you, and whiz right on up the corporate ladder instead.
- You may validate your decision that freelancing is the only way to go for you.
- You can build a portfolio and make a living while you're doing it.
- You'll get a chance to write many types of projects, more than if you waited for them to come to you. You'll find some suit you better than others.
- You'll build a professional network. My first freelance clients were people I'd met in my corporate jobs.
- Your corporate or agency career move gives you the view from the other side of the fence, a good perspective to have, once you start selling to that side.
- It's fun. If you connect with the right company, you may get to travel. Even if you pull trade show duty, it's a chance to go to some fun places and get out of town on someone else's nickel.

Steady, well paying clients aren't going to hire a freelance writer right out of college or with no experience, so take a few years to learn about the real B2B world and enjoy the time you spend doing it.

# APPENDIX B
# Some Marketing Resources

---

**B2B Marketing**

- Advertising Age
  (www.btobonline.com/)
- The B2B PR Blog
  (http://b2bprblog.com/)

**Content**

- Content Marketing Institute
  (info@contentinstitute.com)
- Content Marketing Today
  (http://contentmarketingtoday.com)
- Content Rules
  (http://www.contentrulesbook.com/)

**High Tech Marketing Communications**

- HighTech Communicator
  (http://hightechcommunicator.typepad.com)

**Marketing**

- HubSpot
  (http:/www.hubspot.com)
- Marketing Profs
  (http://www.marketingprofs.com)
- Moz - Inbound Marketing
  (http://moz.com/)

**Marketing Gurus (Just a Sampling)**

- Ardath Albee
  (ardath@marketinginteractions.com)
- Ann Handley
  (http://www.annhandley.com/)

- Diana Huff
  (http://www.diannahuff.com/)
- David Meerman Scott
  (http://www.davidmeermanscott.com/)

**Online Marketing Groups/Forums - LinkedIn**

- B2B Technology Marketing Community
  (http://www.linkedin.com/groups/B2B-Technology-Marketing-Community-43707/about)
- Inbound Marketers - For Marketing Professionals
  (http://www.linkedin.com/groups/Inbound-Marketers-Marketing-Professionals-21005)

**Presentations**

- R. Altman & Associates
  (http://www.betterpresenting.com/)
  (http://www.betterpresenting.com/the-book/) - download a free PDF of "*Why Most PowerPoint Presentations Suck and How You Can Make Them Better*" by Rick Altman
- Death by PowerPoint
  (http://www.slideshare.net/thecroaker/death-by-powerpoint)
- Nancy Duarte
  (http://www.duarte.com/)
- Presentation Zen
  (http://www.presentationzen.com/)
- SlideShare Blog
  (amit@slideshare.com)

**Social Media**

- TopRank® Online Marketing
  (http://www.toprankblog.com/)
- Social Media Examiner
  (http://socialmediaexaminer.com)

**Taglines**

- chom chom advertising (http://www.chomchomadvertising.com/360-most-famous-business-taglines/) Doesn't matter what your generation, you'll find something here to make you smile.
- DailyBlogTips (http://www.dailyblogtips.com/the-best-website-taglines-around-the-internet/) Snarky, clever taglines from websites.
- TAGL!NEGURU (http://www.taglineguru.com/) Actually a lot of good info about the tagline process.

**Trade Shows & Conferences**

- Content Marketing World - Content Marketing Institute (http://contentmarketingworld.com/)

**Training**

- Steve Slaunwhite - Copywriting Training (steve@copywritingtrainingcenter.com)

Made in the USA
Charleston, SC
18 January 2015